EVERYTHING YOUR KIDS WISH YOU KNEW ABOUT OWNING A BUSINESS

EVERYTHING YOUR KIDS WISH YOU KNEW ABOUT OWNING A BUSINESS

Lessons from Generations of Entrepreneurship

Adam J. Williams, JD/MBA

Copyright © 2024 by Adam J. Williams

All rights reserved. No part of this publication may be reproduced, distributed or transmitted in any form or by any means, including photocopying, recording, or other electronic or mechanical methods, without the prior written permission of the publisher, except in the case of brief quotations embodied in critical reviews and certain other noncommercial uses permitted by copyright law. For permission requests, write to the publisher, addressed "Attention: Permissions Coordinator," at the email address below.

Adam J. Williams
adam@iamadamwilliams.com
https://www.iamadamwilliams.com

Everything Your Kids Wish You Knew About Owning A Business, Adam J. Williams —1st ed.

CONTENTS

1. The Hidden Challenge of Entrepreneurship 1
2. The Transformation 11
3. Three Mindset Shifts 25
4. How to Avoid the Drift 39
5. Surviving Failure 49
6. See Opportunities in the Danger 59
7. Find a Way or Make One 65
8. Know Your Numbers 77
9. The Necessity of Hiring Experts 83
10. Balance is Bullsh*t 91
11. Entrepreneurial Kids - The Next Generation 95

About the Author 101

CHAPTER 1

The Hidden Challenge of Entrepreneurship

Wake up at 4am. Drink a gallon of water. Work out intensely for 2 hours. Meditate for 90 minutes while updating your social media accounts. Skip lunch. Slam an energy drink. Hustle. Grind. Sleep for 47 minutes. And do it all again tomorrow. That's it. That's the secret to success. *Except* that sounds horrible to me. And completely unrealistic. How about this?

Unconsciously hit the snooze button on the alarm that's been going off for 6 minutes, with the noise that somehow entered your dream. Step on a Lego as you go to shut off the alarm that you strategically placed on the other side of the room. Try to take a sip of water from the empty glass on your nightstand. Drop your phone on the floor and wake up your spouse. Spill your first cup of coffee and stain your socks. Realize the kids are going to be late for school. Take one deep breath. Make breakfast. Get out the door. Realize you forgot your phone. Try to keep your employees, clients, landlord, and family happy.

One of the biggest challenges to being an entrepreneur is that you also have to be a human being. Most of us started our businesses so that we could have more freedom, make more money, and stop working so hard so that our bosses get all of the upside.

And after a while of being self-employed, we realize that starting a business has given us even less time and freedom. You may find that for the number of hours you are working, we end up making slightly less than minimum wage. You have become a prisoner to your business.

Before you took the leap to launch your business, you were likely trapped in a 9 to 5, working for someone else. You dreamed of the day you would be your own boss, determining your own schedule and making way more money. Finally, you would have more time for family and friends. You could take vacations as you please—you're the boss, after all. You would have the ultimate freedom to control your destiny rather than operating on someone else's schedule.

But now, months or years into running your business, reality sinks in. You realize a business is like a baby (or a puppy). Just as a new parent cares for their child around-the-clock, with no focus other than meeting the baby's needs, an entrepreneur has a 24/7 focus on keeping the business running. Or like the puppy, it's ruining your rugs and destroying your valued possessions but still getting unconditional love.

To stay afloat, you feel like you have to prioritize your business over friends, family, and your own physical and mental health. You never get enough sleep, you can't keep up with a fitness routine, and you eat quick meals on the go. You have to turn down invites to birthday parties, dinners with friends, and cookouts with the neighbors. You can't remember the last time you've had a chance to have a date night with your spouse. And if you're a parent, it can be devastating to tell your kids that you won't be able to make the big dance recital, soccer game, or even the family dinner at home because you're burning the midnight oil. Any why isn't there enough money in the bank account?

Your business has taken over your life, likely in a more daunting and overwhelming way than your 9 to 5 career ever did. Your leap of faith from your job to starting your business wasn't a leap from working for someone else to unbelievable freedom… It was just a leap from a job to an even worse job.

Sometimes, when I dig into an entrepreneur client's finances, we'll discover that for the amount of hours they're working, they'd make more money and get more benefits if they got a job at Target. The business has turned into a sh*tty job, no better than working retail.

Do you take vacations? If the answer is "Yes, but I'm still checking my email and responding to customers," you don't have a business, you have a sh*tty job. You aren't taking vacations… You're just working from a different place. In 2017, I took my family to Disney World for the first time. When I got back from my vacation, I asked my employees, "How did you do without me?" One of them turned to me and said, "Dude… It was like you never left. You weren't on vacation, you were just working from Disney."

She was right… I remember answering emails and taking client calls while standing in line for rides. Here I was, thinking I was having the time of my life taking my family to Disney, but I never took a break from work. I had come back to the office even more stressed because I hadn't taken a real vacation, I didn't get a real break, and I regretted not being fully present with my family during this milestone in my son's childhood. I was completely burned out.

This wasn't the life I envisioned when I started my business. Something had to change…

The Problem With Hustle Culture

Why do so many entrepreneurs become trapped, working constantly with no attempt to change their lifestyle?

I blame hustle culture. If you're an entrepreneur, the message you're constantly fed is "You just have to hustle and grind to succeed." Yet most entrepreneurs stuck in the "hustle and grind" mindset don't succeed… They just hustle and grind until they burn out. Remember the old adage "Work smarter, not harder"? Hustle culture has tossed this mantra aside.

Now, entrepreneurs see hard work as a badge of honor. We love to brag about how much we struggle, how busy we are, and how the grind never stops.

"Yeah, I worked until 2am and woke up at 5am to head to the office. That's just the hustle, man."

Really? That's something to brag about?

That sounds miserable.

This mentality is completely misguided. We view struggle as a point of pride and feel guilty when success comes too easily. Sometimes, when success comes easily, we self-sabotage and try to make our task more difficult so we can tell others how we fought tooth and nail to get where we are. We want to feel as though we've "earned" success. If I had to guess, I'd say for most entrepreneurs, this feeling comes from a place of insecurity… We're afraid that others will think we don't deserve our success unless it was hard won.

Our culture has trained us to be embarrassed about success. "Shame on those rich folks who have it easy," we think. How many times have you heard people justify their success? For example, your neighbor has a brand new car sitting in his driveway. "Nice car," you tell him. Immediately, he jumps into a justification: "Oh, thanks, the interest rate on financing was really low." Why does he have to downplay his success? Why can't he own the fact that he was successful enough to afford a new car? Who is he afraid of offending?

The idea of "pulling yourself up by your bootstraps" is deeply ingrained into American culture. In this country, we value hard work to a fault. Stubborn and prideful, we keep hustling and grinding until we get what we want, convinced that hard work is the only way to get it. But what if there was a better way?

What if we took a more strategic approach to entrepreneurship that focused on leveraging experts rather than trying to run a business solo? What if we assembled a great team who helped us achieve our vision? What if it didn't have to be so challenging?

Instead of hiring experts to help us, most entrepreneurs want to do everything in our business ourselves because it makes our egos feel good. But that's not a sustainable way to grow a business.

For most entrepreneurs, it's an awareness issue. They don't believe it can be any other way. They don't believe it's possible that the business can work for you instead of you working for your business. They haven't met many people who have actual freedom from their business because they are sitting in rooms with other entrepreneurs commiserating about how hard it is rather than learning from those who have achieved real success.

Or maybe they believe they can't afford to hire anyone. If you're barely making ends meet now, how can you afford the added expense of payroll? But I believe entrepreneurs can't afford to *not* hire anyone. I understand part of being an entrepreneur is working with limited resources, but the reality is your time is the most limited resource there is. You need to be intentional about how you use your time so that you can use it to make more money. But if you fill your time with tasks that don't move the business forward and that could be easily outsourced to someone else, it will be virtually impossible to grow the business. You'll be stuck forever, until you quit, or die.

A final word on hustle culture: hustling and grinding isn't inherently wrong. An entrepreneur needs to be willing to hustle and grind. But the difference is that a successful entrepreneur sees hard work as a means to an end. A successful entrepreneur is willing to hustle for a short time to accomplish a specific goal. Sometimes, the machine needs to be built, but it should be operated by someone other than you so you can focus on building the next, bigger, better machine. Hustling and grinding as a lifestyle sucks.

Entrepreneurs become trapped when they start hustling for its own sake, to feel "busy" and boost their egos. "Hustling and grinding" isn't a sustainable lifestyle. No one should fill their schedules with constant hard work until they die. Instead, the mindset should be, "I need to hustle and grind until __ happens." The end goal of entrepreneurship is to stop hustling and achieve real freedom, but to reach this stage, you will have to put in work along the way. And you need to learn how this can be accomplished.

> **A Wake-Up Call**
>
> Around the same time I was building my law practice, I met a CPA around my age who was building his own firm. I've never had so much in common with someone in my life… We'd gone to the same college, we were at the same point in our careers, and we had kids around the same age. We both loved helping entrepreneurs and would send clients to each other. We even looked alike—one time, his mom tapped me on the shoulder thinking it was her son. We were both working hard to build our businesses and trying to balance raising our young families. It seemed like we were both on the path to success.
>
> One weekend, I was out mowing the lawn when he was driving past on the way to get pizza with his son. He saw me and stopped to chat. We drank a beer and he met my daughter, who had just been born. That was the last time I saw him. Two weeks later, he said goodbye to his pregnant wife and young son, drove to his office, and killed himself.

The shock of my friend's suicide propelled me to examine my own life. If someone who was living a nearly identical life to my own was driven to that point, what could I do to ensure I wouldn't have a similar fate? I went to a therapist for the first time and began making a conscious effort to focus on my mental and physical health. I quickly accepted that the long hours and endless stress of running my business would lead to burnout. I could no longer live my life that way—and no entrepreneur should have to, either. I needed to make a change. But I had no idea where to start.

I invested in a coaching program and began to learn how to work on the business instead of in the business. Talking to other business owners, I realized that it was possible to have a business that works for you instead of working for your business. I remember one entrepreneur got on the stage and said, "I have a $700,000 law firm." At the time, I thought, "Wait…That's not even possible." I was making half of that, working constantly, and had maxed out my credit card just to attend this coaching session. Later in the program, I met dozens of law firm owners who were making millions a year in revenue—and not working 24/7 to make it happen. I began to open my eyes to what was possible, and the transformation began.

A single-shareholder law firm that generates $300,000 in revenue is respectable. I couldn't have built that without the experience and education I got from my entrepreneurial parents. But as I continued on my journey, learning my own lessons, I've now built a $5 million business. I'm doing it about 4 blocks away from the poorest zip code in the country, in one of the least entrepreneurial cities in America.

Four years later, I'm sitting in a cabin on the shores of Lake Michigan on a Tuesday morning writing this. My 20+ employees are running the business while I am away, and I can focus on sharing some of my hard-earned wisdom and experience with you, dear reader.

If I can do it, so can you. The lessons in this book are intended to help you supercharge your growth and success.

These are the lessons I want my children to learn when they start their careers or businesses. I hope to save you months or years of heartache, difficulty, and disappointment and help you achieve the freedom and income you previously dreamed of.

CHAPTER 2

The Transformation

Entrepreneurship has been in my DNA since birth. My parents owned a business, and my dad worked his tail off. He bought into the mindset of "If you want to make more money, work harder," and it worked for him. He was the best in the world at what he did, and he had the trophies to prove it.

I was always interested in business because I grew up around it. My parents never had a traditional job that I saw. We always put in the effort to shop local. We always believed we controlled our own destiny.

I remember the first time I got bit by the entrepreneurial bug. I was in 3rd or 4th grade, and Sam's Club sold gumball machines. I convinced my parents to front me the seed money. I bought a machine and some gumballs and had my first business set up in their shop. I eventually scaled from that gumball machine to an M&M dispenser, a snack vending machine, and a soda vending machine in their shop, plus another gumball machine in a friend's store. Fortunately, they didn't charge me for driving me around to pick up supplies and retrieve my money, but this was an early lesson in inventory management, product placement, and, frankly, theft.

In college, I got an internship working for one of those college painting businesses. There, I learned sales and marketing, I learned hiring and firing, and I learned budgeting. It was a crash course in running a business. When the internship was done, I decided to start my own house painting business while taking summer classes. I remember sitting in a public speaking class in college while two different crews in two different locations in the city were making me money. I was able to pay my own tuition through the money I made from that business. I would swipe my credit card at the beginning of the semester and work to pay it off by the end of the semester so I could do it again next time.

Around this time, I also worked with my dad to expand his consumer electronics business. We set up a kiosk in the mall selling remote car starters. I would sit in the kiosk and when the mall wasn't busy, I had time to study. It was the holiday shopping season, and I probably sat in that kiosk for 100 hours per week. I actually ended that semester with a 4.0 because I had so much free time to study.

When I graduated, I made the decision to go to law school and added an extra semester to get my MBA. My dad wanted me to do what he never did: get a nine-to-five salary job with a Fortune 500 company, have a predictable income, have benefits for the rest of my life, and retire with a fat retirement account.

Feeling the weight of my dad's advice, I applied for jobs after graduation and ended up at a Big Four accounting firm. I was working with great people on challenging projects…but the work was completely uninspiring to me.

I stayed at that job for 366 days, just long enough to keep my signing bonus, which I had used to pay for my bar prep.

My wife and I moved back to our hometown, and I ended up taking a clerkship position with a judge. Though I'd been to law school and passed the bar, I knew little about practicing law, so it was fascinating to watch so many lawyers in court, and I became connected to many small firm lawyers in Erie. After about a year, I decided to start my own firm as a side hustle.

I hustled, and it took me 6 months to find enough work that I could quit my job and replace my income. I began working in an office space with several other solo firm owners. It was a collection of lawyers that shared building expenses, but we were each essentially self-employed, though our names were on the same letterhead. My first clients came from a Craigslist ad, and they still work with our firm today.

I would take every crappy referral from every lawyer I met… If they didn't like the client or didn't think the case was worth anything, they'd send it to me and I'd do it. In hindsight, it was a great experience because I learned so much about so many areas of the law, from juvenile delinquents to prenups, to business law.

Whether I was working late or going in on weekends, I would see the other solo firm owners at the office. Everyone was caught in a "hustle and grind loop." They had kids. They had bills. They had vacations planned and needed to work extra hard before and after to afford some time away.

I'd grown up with the perception that lawyers make a lot of money… But I watched these solo firm owners work their tails off and never make great money. My parents, who were entrepreneurs who sold car stereos, made more money than these lawyers. The lawyers in my office had a saying, "Do a good job at a fair price, and you'll always have enough work."

That's true, but I realized I wanted more than just "having enough work." That wasn't the standard I was striving for. After about five years in that office, I decided to go out on my own.

When I began my firm, I had the mentality that every problem could be solved by hard work. If something needed to be done, I would do it. I remember I was quoted a price of $1,300 to have an electrician wire our new office for Internet. Instead of paying the expert, I thought, "How hard can it be?" So I did it myself to save the $1,300. Even for something as mundane as the office running out of toilet paper, I would be the one running to the store. I would bring my kids in on the weekend so I could vacuum the floors and clean the glass. Somewhere in there, I also found time for client work. As I write this, and as you read it, it's easy to see the lunacy in it all, yet I know that many business owners do the same thing.

The American Bar Association says that the average solo attorney bills around 1.2 hours per day. This is because of all of the other "stuff" that needs to get done to operate a law practice. I was able to exceed this average, but it meant bringing my kids into the office way more than they wanted.

As a young lawyer, I gained a great reputation and would consistently get referrals. Unfortunately, all of the referrals were to me and not to my law firm. I had to do all the client work, and I struggled with the idea that in professional services it's difficult to delegate work because people want to hire a specific lawyer, not a law firm. I used that as an excuse for why I couldn't delegate client work. So, I put in more hours. I made the sacrifices I believed I needed to make. I was hustling and grinding.

My son went to a nice preschool near my office, and I would drop him off each morning wearing a suit and driving a Jeep Wrangler that was falling apart. One time, the doors froze shut, and I didn't have power locks. I climbed in through the rear window in my suit. I'd see the other parents showing up in sweatpants driving brand-new Suburbans and Escalades and think, "What am I doing wrong here?" I wasn't intentionally trying to be frugal. I was just getting my a** kicked by life.

How could I make enough money to be driving a swanky car and also have a relaxed lifestyle that meant I could roll up to the preschool in casual clothes instead of rushing to the office? I told myself these people must simply have family money. I consoled myself by feeling superior toward them. "I'm working hard, and they're not. I'm earning my money." Deep down, I knew I was just telling myself a story because I was afraid to face the fact that I was running my business the wrong way. I had created a really sh*tty job for myself.

I had a mistaken belief that if I kept doing what I was doing, everything would someday work out. I thought I needed to power through and keep working hard. But you know what they say, "If you do what you've always done, you'll get what you've always gotten." Or, put another way, what got you here will keep you here.

When my friend committed suicide, I knew immediately that something had to change, but I continued to believe that I could figure everything out on my own.

I had a plan to rent a cabin for two days between Christmas and New Year's so I could do my strategic planning for the year. A friend from law school called around Christmas and asked what I was up to lately, and I told him I was working my a** off so I could get ahead with work and be able to take two days off between Christmas and New Year's. I asked him what he was up to. He said, "Oh, I'm at the Denver Airport with my wife and daughter. We're flying to South Africa for 30 days." I wondered what my kids would think if they knew how this guy was living.

What? I thought. *How is he able to take 30 days off, while I have to work like crazy to be able to take 2 days off to do strategic planning for the business? What does he know that I don't know?*

I discovered that he was hiring and learning from experts. He was getting advice from people who had done what he was trying to do. He wasn't muscling through and trying to figure it all out on his own. He was learning from others and not having to recreate the wheel at every turn. I got him to recommend a coaching program, and I spent the next four years absorbing as much as I could and implementing what I learned. I continued to invest in other programs, spending time with people with more successful businesses and getting over the B.S. stories I was telling myself.

It was hard work… But instead of working hard on client work, I was working hard on building lasting processes and systems for the business. The hard work accumulated, and finally, I had a $5 million business with 20 employees and the ability to take time away from the business whenever I wanted.

Year One - 2019

In 2019, I decided to start treating my practice like a business, not a job. This was the first year I actually wrote a business plan. I got a better grasp of my numbers and began to hold employees accountable. This felt like moving from Kindergarten to 8th grade.

My wife ended up quitting her job at a big bank to come work at the firm with me. She worked a lot of hours and had good benefits at that job, and there was a lot of stability. But we had enough faith in what we were building for her to walk away.

Fortunately, or unfortunately, we also both possessed the "do it all" mindset. Jackie earned the nickname "grout" because she filled in so many gaps in the firm.

The changes we made are obvious in hindsight but, at the time, felt difficult. For example, instead of billing my clients every month, I used to send bills sporadically, mostly when I needed the cash. I would go two or three months without billing, so it was often hard to collect. Then, I implemented a system for consistent billing, and suddenly most of my collection problems (and my cash flow problems) went away.

By the end of that year, we doubled the business. But there were still issues, and we were still suffering from the mindset that we had to do everything.

Year Two - 2020

In 2020, we faced the unexpected challenge of the pandemic. Thanks to all of our professional development training, we were able to go into the pandemic with the mindset of looking for ways to help people and trusting that the money would come later. We adopted the approach that if our clients did better, we would do better. I didn't know "how" I would do it, but I had faith that I would figure it out.

We built marketing campaigns and did webinars, cultivating my presence as a thought leader in our niche - helping businesses through the pandemic.

2020 was also the year we started to learn the value of systems. We developed a path for client intake so we could track where people were in our funnel. We had a salesperson. We figured out how employees were overwhelmed or where we had bottlenecks, and we addressed them.

We grew 50% that year and began to see hints of future success. I did a webinar for the first time, and I made an offer at the end of the webinar for people to buy a small product I created—a set of legal templates. In that one day, we did $35,000 in sales. In one day, we made as much as I made as a law clerk in 2010. We didn't make that every day, but it was an indicator of what was possible. Here we were, in the spring of 2020, when the rest of the world was in chaos, having a record-setting month. Something was working...

Year Three - 2021

In 2021, we focused on more coaching--getting into the room with people who were where we wanted to be.

I could be in a room with other $250,000 business owners, and we could all talk about the problems we have in common. But what would be more valuable is sitting in a room with $1,000,000 business owners and observing how they think and what they're doing differently. And I assure you, they are doing things differently.

One of the things I learned is that the biggest opportunities emerge in times of chaos. That's when people are looking for solutions to calm the chaos. That year, we identified an opportunity born out of the chaos of the pandemic to help businesses claim the new employee retention credit offered by the Federal government. We were one of the first companies to offer that service on a contingency basis. It was a huge opportunity.

Yet 2021 was not without its challenges… In a single month, half of our team quit because they were uncomfortable with how we were growing and changing (or because they thought I was a relentless jerk). This is when "what got you here won't get you there" really hit home for me. I knew the prior version of our team couldn't help us grow a multi-million dollar business, I just had to survive that turbulence.

We could have stopped growing the business at that point, and said, "This is really uncomfortable and difficult. Let's stay where we are so we don't lose any more employees." We lost money that month, which was rare.

But we decided to keep climbing the mountain. If some of our employees didn't want to come with us, they could leave, but we weren't going to stop growing just because our employees weren't comfortable with it. We were seeing progress. Our monthly revenue continued growing, our bank account balance was increasing, but those were both a byproduct of the fact that we were having a bigger impact.

That year, I developed as a visionary and leader, becoming more confident in what I was building. Employees need to buy into your business's vision, but you can't sacrifice your vision for employees that just aren't the right fit. Our mindset at the time was "How do we make our clients more successful?" Some of our employees weren't interested in learning new things to fulfill that mission, so they left, and that was okay—we would keep going.

Year 4 - 2022

In 2022, we faced a decision point: "Do we keep going, or do we shut the business down?" We had built employee retention credit service on a contingency-fee model, meaning we did the work for clients and then waited…and waited…for the government to pay our clients the credit. We had done a lot of work, but it hadn't started cash flowing. Here I was, about a decade into the business, questioning if I even wanted to continue doing it. When I sat down and thought about what we had built and the potential for where it could grow, we decided to keep going.

2022 ended with a milestone. It was the first year we broke $1 million in revenue. We made $1.8 million, which more than doubled the prior year, and we were really profitable! When we sent our numbers to our tax preparer, the only thing he could say was "Wow!"

This was the first year we hired a firm administrator (COO) to run the day-to-day operations of the business so I could focus on higher-level tasks. That was terrifying because I had to let go of some of my authority and trust someone to run my business. This is a stopping point for many people because it gets *very* uncomfortable. But keep reading to find out if it was worth the discomfort…

That year, I also became much more willing to test ideas and risk failure in order to learn. For example, we would put money into a marketing campaign that we weren't sure would work. Previously, we weren't able to risk an idea not working because we needed the cash. But in 2022, we had enough money that we could launch ideas and use it as a learning opportunity to see what ideas worked. And we have lots of lessons on "failure" later in the book.

We continued to improve at tracking our numbers and began to track leading indicators, open rates, click through rates, sales conversions, average client value, and more. The more we paid attention to these numbers, the better the business performed, and we learned what buttons we could push to improve results.

Year Five - 2023 (The Present Day)

In 2023, the year I'm writing this book, everything we spent the last five years implementing has paid off. Our *profit* this year will be multiple seven figures thanks to decisions we made in the past.

We're now better equipped to handle problems, so I can take more risks and make decisions without fear. Every year, I ask myself, "If I lost it all, how long would it take me to make it back?" Each year, the answer gets shorter and shorter, and I'm confident there's more of a safety net when it comes to making decisions.

As the business grows, your problems don't go away, but you get better at handling better problems. It used to be that if a client stiffed me for $1,000, it would be a catastrophe because I needed that to make payroll, but now merely a nuisance that needs to be handled… Now, my problems look like, "I have two great candidates for a job, and I have to decide which one to hire." That's a fantastic problem to have… The problems I have now are situations I would have hoped and prayed for ten years ago. It used to be that my Jeep would have pieces falling off when I shut the door, but now I have to find time to take my Porsche in for an oil change. We have become better equipped to handle better problems.

It's important for you to know that I don't tell you this to brag or show off. Rather, I'm telling you this to show you it's possible, that life does get better. If you are struggling now, you can make the changes you need to live the life you want.

And here's an important note. I'm not special. You, too, are capable of achieving huge success. My hope is that you can do it bigger and faster than I did, and with fewer bumps and bruises along the way.

This year, I had three employees leave (or get fired) before I was scheduled to leave for a two week vacation in Europe with my family. I was still able to take the vacation, the firm made money while I was gone, and I didn't check a single email. The team ended up hiring 6 new employees while I was gone (three to replace those who had left, and three to fill new positions we created because we were growing). When I got back from my trip, I met new employees who had already been working for me for a week.

Learning how to delegate to others is still a process, but I'm able to let my business run without me in ways I would have never imagined were possible.

Some of these lessons I learned as part of an entrepreneurial family. Some of these lessons I learned the hard (and expensive) way. But all of these lessons will help you grow a real business, with real freedom and time for the things you love. In the rest of this book, I'm going to show you how to get there, too. These are the lessons my kids wish I learned 10 years ago…

CHAPTER 3

Three Mindset Shifts

Before I transformed my business, I had a limiting belief that there was only one way to achieve success. I thought that if I was going to have a successful business, I needed to do it the same way I saw others do it.

Over time, as I studied other successful entrepreneurs, I realized that there's no one right way to do things.

After nearly 30 years of seeing things done a certain way by my parents and their successful friends, my eyes were opened to other possibilities. It was only after I changed my perspective on the topics in this chapter that I realized there's more than one path. And that path can be a whole lot easier.

Before these changes, I was stuck in the mud with my tires spinning. These adjustments allowed me to get out of the mud and get my business shifting into second and third gears.

Before we can move forward, there are three mindset shifts you need to make. These mindset shifts were what propelled my transformation as a business owner.

Shift 1 - How You Make Money

Most business owners start out thinking that you have to trade time for money. Want more money? Work more hours.

This mindset has been ingrained in me since childhood. When I was in the fourth grade, my dad paid me a quarter an hour to help him out (yes, this was significantly below the legal minimum wage). At the end of the afternoon, he handed me a dollar. "Hey, I want more than that," I said. He chuckled and said, "If you want more, work more hours." For a long time, I thought the only way to make money was to work more.

But we all only have 24 hours in a day, so if we're trading time for money, we bump up against a biological limit. "Okay," most people think, "So if I want to make more money, but I physically can't work more hours, I'll charge more per hour."

That's how most lawyers operate with the billable hour. I remember the first time I raised my rates to $200 an hour. It seemed like a big deal until I had a plumber come to the house and realized he was charging the same rate. This is the same blue-collar mentality, just at a higher hourly rate… still selling time for money.

Many lawyers bill by the tenth of an hour… It gets ridiculous. Isn't the hourly billing model a backward way to incentivize work? What if one lawyer is faster or more efficient than another? Or what if he has more experience and expertise? Does that mean he makes less than his colleague?

The billable hour model is broken. It overcompensates the lawyer (or any other service provider) for their inefficiencies and lack of experience and under-compensates them for their expertise. Do you want to pay your lawyer to learn and research? Probably not. It's a necessary part of the job, but not anything a client enjoys paying for. There are a few exceptions to this rule, such as many types of lawsuits where you can never predict how unreasonable an opposing attorney will be, so the time involved can be unpredictable. But, for the most part, businesses, and their clients, are better served with value billing.

Even if you're charging a lot per hour, you're still trading time for money. What if we shifted our thinking so money isn't dependent on time? What if we made money by adding value? The easiest way to make a million dollars is to help someone else make ten million dollars. It doesn't matter how much time it takes.

Pricing should be based on outcome, not effort. You agree to pay me a certain price to help you get a certain outcome. When I deliver that outcome, I get paid, regardless of how long it took me or how hard it was. We are both happy because we both got the results we wanted.

When pricing is based on value, you're no longer tied to the clock. All you need are clients who value the service you provide enough to pay your price.

And value is different for every person. Personally, I value speed of implementation. If a service offered an option to pay extra to cut to the front of the line and get an outcome quicker, I would probably pay for it. Why? This gives me more of my most limited resource: time. Others may value a "hands-off" approach and are looking for a service that can get them an outcome with little to no effort themselves. If you are my plumber, I want you to unclog my drain without my involvement. Some people simply value dollars and are looking for the least expensive service that will get them the right outcome. Unfortunately, such a service rarely exists.

Let's look at an example. If I value my time, I may take advantage of a meal prep service or a private chef, as opposed to cooking meals myself. If I prefer the hands-off approach, when I go to a nice restaurant, I may order the chef's tasting menu so that I don't need to make a bunch of decisions. If I value the lowest price, I can get a meal at McDonald's (or grow my own fruits and vegetables if I really undervalue my time). This isn't to say that any of these options are bad, and my preferences may change from day to day. Also, I'm probably offending a bunch of people with vegetable gardens. But anyone who has grown a cucumber knows that you don't do it to save money, and you have to invest a ton of time into the venture. Chances are, you're doing it because you enjoy it. Very few people make money selling their vegetables, and I bet they never calculate their hourly wage.

To stop trading time for money and begin trading value for money, I had to overcome my long-held belief that money only comes from hard work. I had to let go of the irrational feeling that I didn't "deserve" money unless I put in a lot of time and effort. It turns out that once I find out what I'm good at (and what I enjoy doing), I can turn my expertise into profit.

It finally clicked for me when we made $35,000 in a day after our webinar. We had created a spreadsheet to calculate PPP loan forgiveness and sold it for $500. When I watched the spreadsheet sales come in, I realized that people truly valued this spreadsheet. It was an important tool for them that they were willing to pay $500 for because it solved a problem they had. It didn't matter how long it took our team to build the spreadsheet. What mattered is that we had created something that was helpful to people. They were willing to trade dollars for this product that would make their lives easier, even though it cost almost zero additional dollars to sell an additional spreadsheet.

Before that day, I still believed that in order to have value, something had to take sacrifice, hard work, and time. It seemed unfair for someone to be able to make money without putting in time and hard work. That's the old-school, American, blue-collar work ethic. And it was keeping me broke. Since making this shift, we have had single days where our firm collects six figures of revenue. Our little business has days where we generate more than the average small business does in an entire year. All because we focus on charging for the value we provide.

Have you ever had a plumber come to fix a leak by showing up for five minutes, turning a knob, and then charging $150? Five dollars was compensation for the time and effort it took him to show up to your house. But $145 was for knowing what knob to turn to stop the leak. We're all willing to pay the plumber because he stopped the leak. Whether it took him 5 minutes or 4 hours, *all we care about is the outcome*. We should apply this mentality in more areas of our lives and not begrudge those who provide fast or efficient results.

In your work, every client comes in with a problem they need to solve. If you solve that problem, they'll be happy to pay you regardless of how much time it requires. They're paying for the result. Your value is knowing what knob to turn—applying your expertise to the problem. Sometimes, knowing what knob to turn looks like delegating the problem to your team and building a business with systems and processes that set everyone up for success.

Shift 2 - Stop Feeding Your Ego

If you look at what the average entrepreneur does in a week, how many of these actions actually have a benefit and how many are just done to boost the entrepreneur's ego?

Everything you do and every decision you make should have a benefit in one of three areas:

- Does it give you more time?
- Does it make you more money?
- Does it increase the impact your business has?

If it doesn't have a clear benefit other than boosting your ego, don't do it. Stop focusing on things that make you feel good, that allow you to hide out in your busyness, or that don't actually move the needle on your goals related to time, money, and impact.

Many entrepreneurs name their business after themselves because it makes them feel good. But is that the best name for the business? Is there a name that could help the business make a bigger profit or have a bigger impact? Almost always. Rather than making it easy for potential customers to understand what you do and whom you help, we throw our initials in the business name and start ordering embroidered polo shirts and business cards. It takes a lot more time, and a lot more money, to build a business that way.

Think about the new business owner who gets a fancy logo designed, prints it on T-shirts, hats, pens, and stickers, and hands out this merch to all their friends. That feels nice…but does it really move the business forward? Could the time, money, and energy spent on this be spent in a way that benefits the business? No one has ever hired my business because we have really nice pens (even though we do have really nice pens). Rather, we use the fancy pens as a way of enhancing our customer experience. Would you want to sign a million dollar contract with a Bic? Probably not. Would you ever hire a lawyer, coach, or tax strategist because you picked up their fancy branded pen off of a restaurant table? Gosh, I hope not.

I used to feel good about myself for serving on non-profit boards. I noticed I would subtly brag about it: "Oh, yeah, I'm just coming from a board meeting." But I realized that my contributions weren't truly having an impact. I was there because I wanted to make a difference, but I wasn't actually making a difference, because these organizations often don't want to make necessary changes. Going to the meetings was only an ego boost and a waste of time. If I really wanted the outcome of making an impact, I would be better off looking for another way to do that or finding an organization more open to my suggestions.

I used to order new business cards every six months because I had a new idea to make them cooler. But the business cards never made us any money. Most of the time, they sat in a box. It was just an ego booster…so it had to stop. I learned that the only reason I have a business card is so that I can get the other person's business card, and I will follow up with them. Same with radio ads… I love hearing my voice on the radio, but I don't think we got a single client from radio ads, so we have to put our marketing dollars elsewhere.

Often, your ego tells you that you need to be the hardest working person. You want to be the first one in the office and the last one out of the office to make yourself feel like a hero. But does working harder improve your time, money, or impact? Or would your business actually be more profitable if you worked less and could spend more time on long-term strategic thinking?

To let go of the egotistical desire to be the hardest-working person, I shifted my mindset from taking pride in how hard I worked to taking pride in the results the business accomplished.

In 2018, we helped about 100 clients. In 2023, we helped over 500, and we helped them in bigger ways, resulting in more revenue. My impact would have been limited if I had to do it all myself.

Now, I have a COO who runs the day-to-day operations of the business. To make this transition, I had to make an effort to let go of my ego. I found that he runs the business better than I could in a lot of ways. Does that sting my ego a bit? Yes. Do I sometimes feel the urge to run in and make decisions just to feel important? Yes. But implementing a COO who runs the business better than I could gives me more time, money, and impact, so I rein in my ego and focus on the benefits. I find more ways to make the business grow, including marketing, developing our team, and recasting our vision.

This is a huge challenge for many entrepreneurs. It comes down to identity and control. Most entrepreneurs base their identity around their business. It can be scary to watch it operate without you because you wonder who you are if you're not the one making every decision in your business. And many entrepreneurs fear losing control of the business, so they're wary of letting others come in and make decisions. For years, I was viewed as "just" a lawyer. When I decided to change my identity to visionary entrepreneur, I discovered my true purpose. But delegating decisions doesn't mean giving up control.

Recently, my wife and I went for a ride in a friend's plane. I'm interested in getting my pilot's license, so I was studying what my friend did as he flew the plane. At one point, he turned to me and said, "Want to fly? It's easy until you land." I said, "No, I'm not ready to touch the controls yet…But can you fly over our house so we can take a picture? And then can you fly over the lake?" The rest of the flight, I told him where I wanted to go, and he took me there, all while I sat back and relaxed with my wife. Control doesn't mean your hands are on the controls. It just means you decide where you're headed and let others help you get there. Control is the ability to get things done without having to do them yourself. When you take your hands off the controls, you can get more done because others are doing the work for you.

You'll find that as you go through this process, you'll probably go through three stages. For most of us, we start out being self-employed. In other words, we haven't done much more than create a job for ourselves. A small percentage of us can graduate to a stage where we actually own a small business. This means that your business can make money and your customers can be served without you physically being there collecting the payments or doing the work. Finally, a very small percentage of us will become true entrepreneurs. We will create something that did not exist before and truly change lives with the impact that our business has. Ego can prevent many people from moving out of the first stage.

Take your ego out of the equation and focus on what benefits the business. Use time, money, and impact to filter out what you want to invest your time and energy into. If it doesn't give you more of one of those 3 things, don't do it. Run your decision through these filters. You can learn more about our goal-setting and business planning lessons in the next chapter.

Shift 3 - Find More Win-Win Opportunities

I always thought business was a win-lose proposition. Someone wins and someone loses—and you can't win unless everyone else loses. Whether it was other firms, employees, or clients, I saw everyone else as a competitor that I needed to beat. But what if we looked for more win-win opportunities? What if we tried to find ways for both parties to benefit?

When I started my business, I didn't offer employees health insurance. I thought it made more sense to just pay them more money and let them take care of their own health insurance. But I realized my employees wanted to feel safer and would prefer that I provided health insurance and paid them less. I saw it as a win-win to provide health insurance: the employees got what they wanted, and I ended up saving money!

It's crucial to get a clear understanding of what the other person wants out of a transaction or relationship. You also need to understand why it's important to them. Too often, we make assumptions about both of those things. If you can give them what they want while getting what you want, success comes more easily.

Some employees value working from home. A "win-lose" boss might make everyone come into the office to maximize control over employees' time. Yet a win-win boss knows that as long as the employee accomplishes their goals and hits their KPIs, it doesn't matter if they work from home. The boss wins because they get a happier and more productive employee who gets tasks done, and the employee wins because they get the flexibility to work from home, which can make managing work and family life easier.

With a win-win approach, sales shift from being transactional to being about relationships. In the past, it was our goal to close deals as quickly as possible because we wanted the client's money. But now, it's about, "Can we help this person get what they want? Is this relationship profitable for both of us?" With this approach, sales is about the long-term. If we truly provide value to a client, it's likely they'll come back for more. Sales stops being about one transaction and starts being about building valuable, lasting relationships with clients, where everyone wins.

We used to charge clients a flat fee to set up an LLC. After a few days, we'd hand the clients a pile of papers and say, "Congratulations and good luck." But we realized that most of our clients had no clue what to do from there. They came to us looking for an LLC, but what they really wanted was guidance and help establishing their entire business. This could involve help with insurance requirements, accounting and bookkeeping, contracts, and all of those "quick" questions that someone could spend months Googling. We started a monthly subscription service to help clients with insurance, trademarks, accounting, and everything else that comes along with starting a new company. We increased our average client value by charging more, and our clients were happier because we were giving them the more complete solution they really needed.

Even as a buyer, I used to negotiate transactions with a win-lose approach. I would want to "win" by getting more for less. But now, I've reframed my relationship with money. I started to feel good about handing someone a check for services provided because I got the value I was seeking and they felt satisfied earning their fee.

And while we are on the topic, your rates are probably too low. Most entrepreneurs undercharge. If you raised your rates 25%, what do you think would actually happen to your business? Okay, back to the issue at hand.

During the pandemic, when local businesses struggled, my wife and I made a point to buy dinner at local restaurants that needed our support. This reframed my perception of spending money because I stopped to consider the people behind the businesses. It felt good to give my money to small business owners who were trying to stay financially afloat during a challenging time. Our business allowed us to order our meals and have a positive impact on our small business community. After that, spending money was no longer about "getting the best deal." It was about gladly spending money with people who provided value to my life in some way. Could I have taken advantage of their difficult situation? Yep. And a lot of people did. But at what expense?

A win-win approach allows you to build collaborative, long-lasting relationships that will get both you and others closer to where you want to be.

I could write an entire book on these three mindset shifts. However, you don't really understand them until you experience them. This is where hiring a coach can help. A coach can work with you to break old paradigms and reprogram your brain for success.

I know that sounds a little woo-woo, but I've seen it work too many times, in my own life and in others, to discredit it.

I've worked one-on-one with clients to help them come up with a plan to increase their prices based on the value they provide. That can be a really difficult thing to do (*hello*, imposter syndrome). But without fail, every client who has done it properly makes more money and actually does a better job for their clients. Think about it, how excited are you working for a client knowing you're being under-paid? I can attribute most of the success in my life to shifts in my mindset. If you want more, check out http://www.IAmAdamWilliams.com/ for articles and podcast episodes where we dive deep into mindset work.

CHAPTER 4

How to Avoid the Drift

Imagine waking up a year from now. You have the same business. The same life. The only difference is, you have one less year to live.

This happens to too many people, whether they are entrepreneurs or not. It would be fine if they were happy with the way things are going, but too many people sit around waiting for things to change and get better. It's time to start living and working with intention.

Without clear goals, you'll end up in "the drift." With no clarity or direction, you'll keep cranking away at your work with no idea where the finish line is. And when you're not clear on where you're going, it's easy to lose momentum and give up or waste years of your life.

Once upon a time, I was caught in "the drift." I spent years working my tail off seven days a week with no end in sight. Each April, my tax return would tell me how much money I made, and it was never enough. But I'd just go back to work the next day and keep at it for another year, never zooming out to see the big picture and decide where I was going or what I could do differently. It was like getting onto the highway in a piece of crap car and driving aimlessly.

I always used the excuse that I didn't know what my ultimate goal was. Because I didn't know what I wanted, I kept on doing the same thing. The problem was, I was miserable and broke.

Eventually, I decided to set a goal. One of those "SMART" goals they talk about. Specific, Measurable, Attainable, Relevant, and Time-Bound. Actually, mine wasn't time-bound. Maybe it was just a SMAR goal. I decided I was going to save $100,000.

I had worked for years without any real savings other than a small 401(k). I knew I wanted to have some level of wealth so I wouldn't end up as one of those lawyers working until the day he dies, and I knew having savings and investments would help me get there. Within six months, I accomplished that goal, and it was more than I had ever saved. Once I set the goal, it became easy to accomplish it because my priorities changed. I kept my eye on the prize. To save essentially zero dollars over many years to $100,000 in 6-months was shocking. That's the power of having a real goal.

Once I hit $100,000, I decided that my next goal would be to save $1 million. The simple fact that I had a goal in mind gave my life direction. It wasn't just about working in an endless cycle. It was about working so I could accomplish my savings goals, and when I hit those goals, I would have the financial freedom to set and accomplish more goals.

The $1 million savings goal is only the next right step for me. I know if I can have $1.5 million in investable assets, they can be worth over $6 million by the time I retire. My financial advisor and I did the math. $6,694,357 on my 65th birthday with compounding interest. I would never be able to have a concrete goal like that if I never set the $100,000 goal. I don't believe that's "enough" for me, but it's definitely better than zero.

Creating a Crystal Clear 3-Year Vision

Author Jim Collins coined the term "Big Hairy Audacious Goal" to describe a long-term goal that an organization is moving toward. A BHAG is a vision for 10, 15, 20 years in the future, so it's a little blurry. But as your goal-setting timeline gets shorter, the picture becomes clearer.

I know some entrepreneurs who do this very well. They create compelling BHAGs. Unfortunately, I still struggle with that exercise. It isn't yet clear to me what the dent will be that I put in the planet. Rather than using that as an excuse to avoid setting goals, I just shorten the time horizon.

To avoid the drift, I created a crystal clear 3-year vision. I've painted a portrait (figuratively) of my business in the future. It's like a self-portrait. A Future Self Portrait.

Recently, I sat down with my team and told them exactly what we would be doing on December 17, 2026, which is about three years away at the time I'm writing this book. I told them what our Christmas party would look like, who was there, what we were celebrating… Down to the music we were listening to and what the room smelled like. It's more than a vision. It's a full sensory experience.

The Future Self Portrait is like time traveling, and you can read ours to see for yourself here: https://iamadamwilliams.com/futureself or scan the QR code below for quick access.

After reading it, can you picture it? Do you have any doubt about where we are going? Sure, you can question how we will get there, but when we do, it will feel pretty familiar to all of us.

It would be overwhelming to plan what ten years in the future looks like, but the Future Self Portrait gives you a clear picture of where you want to be three years from now. That makes it easier to decide what your goals are for the next year, six months, 90 days…you know where you're going. Suddenly, you and your team are more focused, motivated, productive, and inspired. You know what the priorities are and if you're making progress.

I've created a Future Self Portrait several times now, and it's almost unbelievable how accurate it becomes. When I focus for three years on accomplishing that vision, it comes true, down to the car I'm driving, the house I'm living in, the type of work I'm doing, the type of clients I have, and the people on my team.

If you can't picture 3 years, try one year. Or maybe 6 months. Or 90 days. Just start somewhere.

A documented Future Self Portrait impacts the team, too. First of all, they can decide whether they want to be part of it or not. Plus, they can imagine where they will fit in.

There are a lot of places where you can go to get a paycheck, and there are a lot of employees who simply want a paycheck. But a Future Self Portrait thinks beyond a paycheck and imagines the impact you and your team want to have in the world. If an employee doesn't want to have that impact and just wants to collect a paycheck, the Future Self Portrait lets them know upfront where the business is headed. If people leave, that's okay—eventually, you want your whole team filled with people who enthusiastically embrace your Future Self Portrait and are willing to work with you toward that goal.

When you have this vision clearly defined, you and your team can ensure you're all rowing in the same direction. And your team will be better able to make decisions without you because they know what the long-term vision is. Instead of knocking on your door every five minutes, they can make decisions based on whether an action will bring the team closer to the vision or not.

It keeps you from drifting, from working endlessly while remaining stuck in the same place.

As an entrepreneur, your Future Self Portrait keeps you focused and eliminates distractions. When you have the future outlined in such vivid detail, there's no question whether you're going to achieve your goals or not because you feel like you're already living in that future to some extent. It's easier to stay committed when you believe your goals are within your reach. On the rough days, you can look at your vision and think, "This is what it's going to be like…It will all be worth it."

There's another benefit as well. We share our Future Self Portrait with clients and vendors. It helps us attract our people, the right type of clients. Our clients know they are part of something awesome, and they *want* to be a part of it.

A Framework for Goal Setting

Go to https://iamadamwilliams.com/futureself for a quick overview video of how the Future Self Portrait works or scan the QR code with your phone to go directly to the video.

Your Future Self Portrait is your overarching target for the next three years. But for the next twelve months, we focus on three categories to set goals: time, money, and impact.

You've probably heard that you should have a written business plan for your business. You may have seen some examples on the internet, or maybe your banker gave you some guidance if you were applying for a loan.

Those business plans are useless. They're typically written for the wrong audience, the format is confusing, and once they're written, they're saved to a folder and never looked at again.

A good business plan will be written for you, as the owner. It should focus on what you want and your plan for how you will achieve it. It should be something that you review at least quarterly, and it should be written in a way that you can easily understand.

Below are the three sections that we use in our business plan. For an additional video resource, as well as a spreadsheet to help you calculate your number, go here: https://www.iamadamwilliams.com/goalsetting and of course, you can use the QR code below to go straight to the video.

Money

Each year, my wife and I sit down to calculate what it costs to live the life we want to live. I know what our mortgage and car payments are for our dream house and our dream cars. If we want to hire a landscaper or housekeeping service, we factor that in. How much do we want to spend on food? How much do we want to spend on travel? How much do we want to give to charity? We cover every spending category until we have a picture of the life we want to be living. Then, we compare it to what we're spending now—and it can be terrifying, because sometimes it's a huge jump. Sometimes it's, "Woah, we're doing fine now, but to live the life we really want to be living I need to make triple what I'm making now." Sometimes, people get scared by this big number and back off. They alter their vision of their dream life, thinking, "I don't really need all of this, do I?" But it's important to allow yourself to dream and not be limited by the cost. When you know how much it costs to live your dream life, you have a number to work towards. You know how many clients you need to make that dream number—and you can begin taking action to move toward that goal.

My number has doubled, then doubled again since the first time I did this exercise. But you know what else has 4x'd? *My income.*

Time

There are only 168 hours in a week. We can't change that. Unlike money, time is limited. How do you want to spend your time in the next 12 months?

I have to make sure there's time for myself, my wife, my kids, and my business. Within each of those categories, I'll break down specifically what time I want to have.

For time to myself, I'll want time to meditate and time to exercise. I'll want time to drink coffee and daydream with my wife in the morning, and I'll want time for date nights and vacations with her throughout the year.

My kids have completely different interests, so I'll want time to spend with each of them doing what they like and time to spend with the whole family together.

Then comes work…What do I want to be doing in the office? I don't want to be the receptionist or even practice law.

I want to spend my time as the CEO, the visionary, the leader. I also want to work on marketing because I enjoy that.

When you get clear about how you want to spend your time at work, it becomes easy to recognize what you can delegate.

If you could design your perfect week, what would it look like? Once you know, you can start building towards it.

Impact

What impact do you want to have? What's the dent you want to put in the universe?

Impact is hard to quantify, but it captures the big-picture purpose that drives your life.

I decided that I want to empower more entrepreneurs to live lives of true freedom.

Once I have my vision of time, money, and impact goals for the year, I can use them as a rule of thumb to decide what actions to take. If an opportunity comes across my desk, I can quickly ask myself, "Will this help me reach the amount of money I need to live my dream life? Will this help me have more time to spend how I want? Will this help me make the impact I want to make?" If it doesn't do any of these three things, I'll turn it down.

Before I had this goal-setting framework, people would ask me what I wanted and I'd say, "I don't know. I'm just going to show up and work every day." This approach left me miserable. But with a vision for the future, every day you're driving toward your dream life until you make it a reality.

Having the plan written can also be a useful tool for visualization. Before I bought my first Porsche, I would imagine what the door sounded like when I opened it, what the seats felt like, and what the exhaust sounded like when I started it up. I know this is more woo-woo mindset stuff, but this exercise allowed me to find that car in my garage sooner than I expected. Professional athletes visualize the perfect play, the perfect putt, the perfect foul shot over and over. You can do the same in your business and life.

CHAPTER 5

Surviving Failure

When I was in grade school, you needed 92% accuracy to get an A, and if you got 68% accuracy or less, you failed. I learned these numbers at 6 years old, in 1st grade. But in business, if you get it right 60% of the time, that's not a failure… You could get it right 60% of the time and still be a multi-millionaire.

Yet so many entrepreneurs, especially those of us who succeeded academically, are still trapped in the "student" mentality that fears failure. We think we need perfection to succeed, and we're afraid of being wrong.

But failure is necessary if you want to be a successful entrepreneur. Without failure, an entrepreneur will never learn what works and what doesn't. It's a vital learning experience that propels an entrepreneur to improve. Who do you think is more knowledgeable, the baseball player with one home run at one at-bat or the player who has struck out 100 times before hitting his first homerun?

So, let me help to clarify things a bit. **There are only 3 ways to fail:**
1. You don't try
2. You don't learn the lesson
3. You quit

You Don't Try

> In President Theodore Roosevelt's famous 1910 "Citizenship in a Republic" speech, he said, "It is not the critic who counts; not the man who points out how the strong man stumbles, or where the doer of deeds could have done them better. The credit belongs to the man who is actually in the arena, whose face is marred by dust and sweat and blood; who strives valiantly; who errs, who comes short again and again, because there is no effort without error and shortcoming; but who does actually strive to do the deeds; who knows great enthusiasms, the great devotions; who spends himself in a worthy cause; who at the best knows in the end the triumph of high achievement, and who at the worst, if he fails, at least fails while daring greatly, so that his place shall never be with those cold and timid souls who neither know victory nor defeat."

The "cold and timid souls" that Roosevelt describes are those who never try—so by default, they have failed.

When I was a kid, my dad took me to a skate park to rollerblade. This place had all sorts of ramps, rails, and half pipes. When I was done, we got in the car, and I said, "Dad, guess what? I didn't fall the whole time." My dad looked at me and said, "Well, you didn't try very hard." That comment hurt more than any fall on a ramp, but he was right… I had been so focused on not falling that I missed the point of being at a skate park. If I pushed myself a little further, I probably would've fallen all over the place, but I would become a better skater by the end of the day and would maybe be able to do cooler tricks. "Not falling" looks like perfection, but it's really just playing it safe. Playing it safe doesn't get you anywhere… It just keeps you comfortable because you feel like you didn't mess up.

It's easy not to fall on your face if you never take any risks. But if you never take any risks, how will you accomplish anything worthwhile?

No newspaper articles are written about the great idea that stayed in someone's head until the day they died.

No statues are built for the person who thought of a better way of doing things but never actually did it.

You Don't Learn the Lesson

As the quote often attributed to Einstein goes, "Insanity is doing the same thing over and over again and expecting different results."

Mistakes are great. They teach you what you could do differently so that next time you can get a better result. But if you keep making the same mistake over and over again without learning a lesson from it that helps you make a different choice…you failed.

You aren't going to get it right on your first attempt. You're going to be slow. You're going to make mistakes. Even if you do have some success, you will discover ways that you could have done it better.

A racecar driver should be faster in the last hour of a practice session than he was in the first hour. He should be figuring out where he was losing speed so he can use a different approach next time. But if he approaches the race in the same way every time, he'll never improve. And if he expects to become faster overnight without changing his approach, he's deluding himself. He will study his line, where he hit the brakes, and where he entered a turn, and during the next session (if he's a professional), he'll do it better. If he kept the same approach every time, his times wouldn't get better. In fact, they'd probably get worse because his tires are wearing out.

The first time I landed a plane with my flight instructor, I almost knocked my teeth out with the bumpy landing. Now, my landings are butter. If I never tried, and faced crosswinds or rainy days, I'd never know the joy of being able to fly my family to new, fun destinations.

Professional athletes have the luxury of practice. They can put themselves out there, with other competitors on the field, and take a lot of shots without the risk of losing a game.

Business owners have to practice during the game. Because of this, it's crucial that we learn from our mistakes and adapt our approaches as we try and fail.

Recently, my family took a two-week European vacation. It was the first time I ever hired a travel agent—and she completely messed up the trip. We got to the airport, and they wouldn't even let us board the plane because she didn't send the correct information. What was supposed to be our luxury vacation with all the planning handled for us turned into a hassle of driving to New York City to go to the passport office for an emergency appointment, finding a hotel for the night, then driving back to the airport and booking a different flight.

If I hired that same travel agent again, knowing how badly she messed up our first trip, that would be a failure because I didn't learn the lesson. But this hassle turned out to be a funny family story. It taught me that I'd better do more research into travel agents I hire and double check our flights with the airport in advance.

You Quit

Quitting is the ultimate way to fail. It's declaring your own failure—that you'll stop pursuing your goal.

But unless you quit, you don't try, or you don't learn the lesson, no matter how many mistakes you make, you haven't failed. In fact, you should celebrate that you are on the path to success. When you reframe failure to just those three categories, mistakes become necessary opportunities for growth that help you on the path to your goal.

I've had my share of "failures" over the years…

During the 2016 Presidential election, some friends and I created *Socialism: The Game*, a satirical version of Monopoly in which the game is over when everyone has the same amount of money. The game quickly got attention in the press. We launched on a Friday, and the next Wednesday we were in Manhattan being interviewed on Fox News. Vice Magazine even did a funny article in which real members of the Democratic Socialists of America played the game, and actually enjoyed it!

But the project was a complete financial failure… I don't think we broke even. Somewhere in Pennsylvania, there's probably a warehouse with 5,000 unsold copies of the game.

But even knowing the project would fail, I would still go back and do it all over again.

For one, it was an incredible learning experience about marketing. We had created a brilliantly playable board game with flawlessly designed rules. The problem was, we shouldn't have been selling this to avid board game players… We were really selling a gag gift that people could use to tease friends and family about their political opinions. If we had recognized this from the start, we could have better strategized our marketing. Now, I'll always look at future endeavors with a better eye to the nuances of how an audience uses a product or service. This was also the first time I'd worked with co-founders, so it taught me about how to navigate working with other leaders, who may have different opinions on how to do things.

On the other hand, the experience was a lot of fun. That hilarious Vice Magazine article is still out there somewhere, and it was cool to watch something that had started as a joke between friends catch the media's attention. I'll always have this venture as my "cocktail party" story to entertain new acquaintances with, and I'll always share the ridiculous memories of this project with my buddies who founded it with me.

That wasn't my only big (perceived) failure by any means… One of my favorite ways to open a speech is, "In 2018, I spent $25,000 on cheese."

The story is, a friend and I had the idea to launch a grilled cheese food truck in our town. We made a little bit of money, and we ended up selling our business to new owners, but it gave me a ton of cool stories to tell and it taught me important lessons about running a business.

When we sold our truck, I remember hearing that a guy I knew made some comment like, "Of course they failed.

They were selling grilled cheese sandwiches for $13." But this guy missed the point completely. Could we have made more money if we did things differently? Maybe. But our selling the truck wasn't a failure. It was us deciding to let go of the project and move on. The new owners now have 2 trucks under the brand, and that troll is on his 4th job and 2nd college degree since then. I still bet I got more of an education.

Recently, I was at an event, and I went up to the window of a food truck to order and saw that it was my former manager. She had started her own food truck after ours was sold. She turned to her employee and said, "This is Adam. Our food truck wouldn't exist if it wasn't for him."

From one person's perspective, we failed because we sold our truck, but we profited greatly from the learning, and we created impact with our employees who, because of the learning experiences they had alongside us, were able to launch their own businesses later on. I wouldn't call that a failure, would you?

I took the lessons I learned on that truck, implemented them in our firm, and now we are one of 4 companies in Erie certified as a Great Place to Work.

Non-entrepreneurs have such a stigma around failure. Often, this causes entrepreneurs to fear failure because of what other people will think of them. Many are afraid to try anything to begin with because they don't want to be judged as a failure if it doesn't work. It's easy to hide in your cubicle or behind your keyboard, never putting yourself on the line for your goals. But if someone judges you for "failing," they just have a fundamental misunderstanding about what failure means.

I once worked with a client to buy out his partners in the doggy daycare business they started together. I found out that the owners were spending their time doing $10 an hour jobs in the business: washing dogs, mowing the grass, cleaning the windows. The business was not profitable…I told them the hard truth that they would all make more money if they got jobs at Target. They were spending a lot of time doing low-level tasks in an attempt to save money, yet they didn't have the profit to show for it. Finally, I said that if you can't afford to pay someone $10 an hour to mow the lawn and groom dogs, you'd better reconsider how your business is set up. I gave them some suggestions for ways they could hire people to take over the low-level tasks so they could focus on finding more dog owner clients.

But they kept operating the way they always had been, and eventually, they went out of business. They lost their investment and destroyed their credit because the bank foreclosed on the building they owned. They could have closed the business much earlier or taken steps to fix it… But they were too prideful. They were afraid to "fail" and admit that the business wasn't profitable and go get other jobs. At the same time, they refused to change the way the business was run. If these business owners had overcome their fear of failure, they could have sold the business before the bank shut it down or course corrected and started to create profit and cash flow.

The truth is, I don't want advice from the person who hits a home run on the first try. That person was probably lucky or merely gifted in an area, but they haven't learned anything. I want advice from the person who tried something 57 times before they got it to work. That person knows all the reasons why something doesn't work and what they had to do to make it work.

My son is obsessed with the NFL, and he likes to make fun of the Buffalo Bills, who lost three Super Bowls in a row in the 90s. "Wait a minute," I told him one day, "They were the second team in NFL history to make it to three Super Bowls in a row. That means three years in a row, they were the second best team in the world. Who are you to call them losers?"

I want to teach my son early on that failure isn't to be feared—it's to be celebrated.

We all celebrate the big investments and big exits, but what if we also celebrated the ideas that didn't work? Sure, my political board game venture and grilled cheese food truck ideas didn't make me a billionaire, but why should I feel ashamed that these ideas didn't pan out? Instead, I want to celebrate that I took a leap and tried something, even if it didn't stick, *and learned valuable lessons that have improved my law firm and my life.*

I celebrate our failed marketing campaigns, our misguided hiring decisions, and the one time we ordered like 30 extra cases of toilet paper by accident. Each of those "mistakes" has given me the opportunity to get better.

I sometimes get asked, "What's your biggest regret?", and I struggle to come up with an answer. Truthfully, I don't regret doing anything. Every mistake I made was a necessary step that taught me a lesson that led me to where I am today.

Rather, I regret the things I didn't do, and the risks I didn't take. That's real failure—sitting on the sidelines afraid to make a move. **Step into the arena.** One of my favorite keynote speeches to give addresses people's attitudes towards failure. It's available on my website at http://www.IAmAdam/Williams.com

CHAPTER 6

See Opportunities in the Danger

"All great changes are preceded by chaos."

-Deepak Chopra

When I was in college in the early 2000s, I asked my dad if he was worried about how the recession would impact his consumer electronics business. Everything in the news talked about how bad things would be for the economy, for businesses, and for people in general.

He said, "No, I just have to make small changes. There's actually a huge opportunity for us. Rather than buying new houses and cars, people are going to fix up the ones they already have." While the rest of the world was freaking out about the economy, my old man was calm, cool, and collected.

He was right... People were going to be more interested than before in buying things like car stereos because they wouldn't have the money to buy new cars, but they wanted nice things. Instead of spending $30,000 on a new car, they'd just spend $500 to upgrade their current one, he thought.

This conversation was a complete paradigm shift for me. As the rest of the world was panicking, my dad, and likely many other successful business owners, were seeing the opportunity to meet people's needs in a new way.

When COVID hit, I followed my dad's approach. Rather than freaking out, my wife and I realized that our business would do better if our clients, most of whom own small businesses, did better. We looked for opportunities to help people and trusted that the money would follow. We discovered that people needed help understanding the new PPP loans, so we focused on adding services around that need and the business grew.

Successful entrepreneurs focus on opportunities, not threats. Circumstances are always changing, and the key is to figure out how to succeed in any circumstance. Simply avoiding threats won't position your business in a proactive place to grow despite challenges.

We had been through this before with our business. When the Dodd-Frank Act passed in 2010, the rules for how to close a residential real estate purchase changed. A lot of lawyers thought it was a burden to learn the new rules, so they didn't bother to adapt. Meanwhile, my wife and I saw the opportunity to figure it out and fill a necessary role in the marketplace. This added a quarter of a million dollars to our top-line revenue when a bunch of older lawyers decided they didn't want to learn new things.

Whether we're talking about global events or small-scale setbacks in the business, we've adopted an approach of seeing opportunities in danger. If an employee leaves, we see it as an opportunity to up-level that position and fill it with someone who's a better fit for the company. If we lose a client, we don't view it as a loss— maybe they weren't a good fit, and now we can spend our time attracting clients who are better long-term fits. Yes, it can be really inconvenient, hurtful, or discouraging when those things happen. But when you're looking for the opportunity, the setbacks are easier to survive.

More than once, I've picked up the phone to call a client who left us a one-star review after working with our firm. There is a lot you can learn from these conversations if you approach it as an opportunity to learn and get better. And more than once, I've helped the client, and they decided to switch it up to a five-star review. What's the catch? I had to get over the terror of calling a pissed off client. I had to swallow my pride and get over the fact that maybe our team screwed something up. It's a harrowing experience, but it's worth it every time.

The Importance of Environment

To see opportunities, you have to put yourself in the right environment. This means making time and space to step away from the "grind" and allow your mind to daydream.

We've all heard of the concept of "shower thoughts." The simple act of being alone with your thoughts in the shower, with nothing to distract you, usually prompts great ideas that wouldn't have occurred to you if you were at your desk checking your email. That "space" that you get during those few minutes in the morning allows you to get creative. Imagine if you intentionally created more of that space.

During COVID, I found that I would get great ideas when I went to the driveway to play basketball with my kids. I worked harder those first few months of the pandemic than I ever have as I tried to figure out how to grow our business.

Stepping away from my desk and doing something active allowed my brain to get a new perspective on the challenges I'd been working on. I can shoot free throws without consciously focusing on it, which gives my mind time to wander and be creative.

This year, I decided to do our firm Leadership Team annual retreat in a cabin in the mountains. We have a nice office in Erie, but I know it'll be valuable for everyone to step away from the day-to-day grind and spend time in a beautiful, inspiring environment.

I remember when I first started as a lawyer, there was a lawyer in my office who people would make fun of because when they walked into his office, he'd have his back turned and be staring out the window. The other lawyers teased him, but this man was coming up with brilliance… and it showed up in the results he got for his clients.

Entrepreneurs need "staring out the window time." We need to carve out time intentionally where we put our phones and computers away and can open ourselves to opportunities and ideas lingering at the back of our minds. Without this time, it's hard to succeed. This may be 15 minutes on a Tuesday, a 3-day vision quest in a nice hotel, or a retreat in a remote cabin. It's crucial for your business to create this space.

Everything around you should be inspiring. Your house, your car, your clothes, the people you surround yourself with… And if your surroundings don't inspire you, rent a beautiful place in an environment that does inspire you. Whether you realize it or not, these elements affect your ability to receive ideas and see opportunities.

And what inspires each person is different. My dad had an office in the basement of his business, and it wasn't a beautiful place by any means, but it was silent and there were no distractions. He also liked to work after midnight because no one was around to distract him.

Personally, I find I'm most inspired in nature. If I need to do deep thinking, I'll rent a cabin in the woods with no cell service, or on a more frequent basis, I'll take my dog for a walk to a remote part of our property. It takes trial and error to figure out what works for you.

Like Henry David Thoreau, I prefer to be in nature. My dad preferred his cave-like office. A few successful clients need the pool at the Ritz Carlton. Find what works for you, but start somewhere.

The goal is to maximize the possibility that you'll have a "lightbulb going off" moment in your daily life so you can see the opportunities that you might have missed if you stuck to the daily grind. This is how you create real value as a visionary entrepreneur. You probably had more time for this before you started your business. Make space to be creative and inspired.

It's important to note that I'm not telling you to take more vacations (although maybe you should). This isn't going to an all-inclusive resort and pounding margs all afternoon. This isn't a trip to Disneyland. This is creating time to think about your business. Contemplate problems. Discover solutions. You need space to be inspired, to find new ideas and opportunities. Start with an afternoon. Sit by yourself and let your mind wander. I suggest a Tuesday afternoon to start.

Once you get these short escapes, and you learn what inspires you to create, then you can start surrounding yourself with more of that in your life.

CHAPTER 7

Find a Way or Make One

In a bacon-and-egg breakfast, the chicken is involved, but the pig is committed.

We went to New Orleans for my dad's 40th birthday. I remember 3 things about that trip. We went to a French restaurant, and the food was horrible. My mom bought a Tommy Hilfiger jacket, and it was so expensive, she justified it by saying she'd share it with me, and my parents bought a piece of art.

Maybe it wasn't really a piece of art, but it was a framed poster of sorts. We found it in the gift shop in the lobby of the Marriott. It was a small sign with a quote on it:

> "We will either find a way or make one"
>
> - Hannibal

The sign has been hanging in my parents' home ever since. That simple phrase has been stuck in my brain since that day in 1992. It's a powerful reminder that if you want something bad enough, you can make it happen.

Over the past 30 years, I've learned that there's a certain level of commitment required if you're going to have an approach like that. Unfortunately, too many people get interested in their success without actually committing to it.

Are you involved or committed? Are you merely a contributor or do you have skin in the game?

One of my mentors taught me that the Latin root of *decide* means to cut off. If you make a decision, you cut off other alternatives. You have skin in the game. There are no alternatives.

In 2019, my wife and I decided to commit to the law firm. We would have no fallback plan and no alternatives but to make the business work. My wife quit her job, where she currently made more money than I was making at the law firm, had amazing benefits, and could work from home four days a week. She left all of that to join the family business.

We were going to find a way or make one. And now, we didn't have my wife's salary to fall back on if the law firm didn't work out. We had decided, and there was no alternative. At first, every time we hired someone, I was worried about making payroll. But we had no choice but to do so every month. We found a way or made one. We've now reached a level of success that we couldn't have imagined in 2019, and that was made possible because of one decision.

The essence of being an entrepreneur is making it work. You find a way to provide value in exchange for the money you need to pay for things like payroll, a mortgage, or a fancy coffee machine. But it's like a muscle that you have to build. The first few times you have to "make it work," it's difficult, but it gets easier each time.

At first, it can be a leap of faith. But once you take the first leap and make it work, you have enough stability that you can make the next leap, and then the next, and the next. It's a compounding effect, and each time, you leap a little further. You build confidence in yourself.

But people often get worried when they don't see the entire path. A path to success is never linear, and it usually won't happen in the way you expect it to. So don't hold yourself back from starting just because you can't see the whole path yet. Map out your first three to five steps and execute on those. Then, stop (or slow down), and re-evaluate.

People hold themselves back from starting because they get caught up in the "how," and if they don't know "how," they don't take action. Just because you can't see the entire path doesn't mean you can't (or shouldn't) start the journey.

Sometimes, you just need to jump off the cliff and build the airplane on the way down. Of course, it's better to have a plan before you make a leap, but sometimes, committing to a decision before you know how you'll make it work is better than taking no action at all.

Process, Not Outcome

A lot of people focus on outcome goals, not process goals.

The most common example of this is weight loss. If someone wants to lose 10 pounds, all they focus on is that outcome. But it's nearly impossible to lose 10 pounds without sticking to a consistent diet and exercise routine. If you frame the goal as being about the outcome of losing ten pounds, you'll give up when you don't see any weight loss. But if you implement healthy lifestyle goals that are process-oriented, like "I'll exercise for 30 minutes per day and I'll cut junk food from my diet," you'll be more likely to maintain this routine and progress. It's about setting goals for actions you want to take, not setting goals for results you want to get. Plus, it's a lot simpler to commit to taking those steps every single day than committing to an outcome.

When you set a process goal, you have to decide that nothing is going to stop you from doing the activities you say you're going to do. If your goal is to exercise for thirty minutes a day, you have to commit to checking that box no matter what. My wife and I have had to do walking workouts in the airport sometimes to meet our exercise goals. But our health, wellness, and fitness have measurably improved.

Another example is sales calls. If you get hung up on the goal of closing one sale, you'll come across as desperate. It would be better to commit to making 3 calls, 5 calls, or 10 calls to the best of your ability. Commit to whatever number it will take to close a sale, rather than committing to just closing one sale.

If you meet your process goal, you'll likely also meet an outcome goal along the way. But the point is that your focus can't be on the outcome. Your focus has to be on consistently repeating habits.

Often, people wait for the "perfect time" to start working on a process goal. They think, "I'll do it after my birthday, after my vacation, after the holidays." But there will always be something in life that gets in the way, so don't make excuses—get started now, and stick to your process goals no matter what the circumstances are.

And if you accidentally miss a day with your process goal, that's not a failure or a reason to quit. Pick it back up the next day.

If you map out a "process plan" for your business and execute that plan every day with no excuses, your odds of success are high. Or after a while, if you're not getting the results you want, it's time to adjust the plan.

Too often, people focus on the outcome, like a revenue goal. If you break that revenue goal down into a number of customers you need at an average purchase price, then to how many sales calls you need to convert that number of clients, then to how many leads you need to get those calls, all you have to do is get the leads.

Early Habits That Started My Transformation

1) I forgave myself for past failures.

A rocket is off track 98% of the time. It's constantly adjusting its course, and it finally lands where it needs to land. When it lands, everyone's impressed. They don't say, "Oh, you stupid rocket, you were off track 98% of the time." I forgave myself for not getting everything 100% right as long as I was heading in the right direction.

2) I let go of my fear of getting it wrong.

I used to be so afraid of setting the wrong goals that I wouldn't set any goals at all. Talk about a failure! But setting the wrong goals isn't the end of the world. A while ago, I thought I wanted to get into woodworking as a hobby. I bought equipment, made a wood shop in the garage, and made plans for things I wanted to build for the house. But I slowly discovered that I didn't enjoy woodworking as much as I thought I did. I would beat myself up for it. "Why aren't you out in the garage? Didn't you want to build that dining room table?" But I just didn't love doing it as much as I thought. I enjoy it as a hobby, but I don't need a massive woodshop for what I wanted to accomplish. I built toyboxes for each of my kids when they were born, and I've built the occasional small table. That's enough for me. My goals changed, and recognizing that it's okay to change a goal was an important epiphany for me. I set the wrong goal, but if I hadn't set that goal, I would have never realized I didn't like woodworking and might have always wondered "What if?" Realizing you need to change a goal is still productive.

Another time, I set a goal to buy one of those Jeep Wrangler trucks, the Gladiator. But when I test drove it, I realized I hated it… It looked cool, but it wasn't great to drive. It rode like… a Jeep. In a past life, I would have been annoyed at myself for choosing the wrong goal, but now I knew that it was okay to change my mind. Or worse, I would have bought the truck just because I had told people I wanted it, and I didn't want to admit I got it wrong.

My wife and I once thought we wanted to have a big residential real estate closing and settlement business. We invested time and money into the goal. We hired employees, bought expensive software, and marketed the practice. But we realized we hated it, so we just stopped doing it. We killed the goal, and that was okay. There was a time when I would have stubbornly stuck to that goal because I didn't want to quit. Actually, back then, I probably wouldn't have even set that goal because I would have wanted to be 100% certain about what I wanted. We ran the business, made some money doing it, but it didn't allow us to spend time the way we wanted to spend it, and we weren't working with the type of people we wanted to work with. We used that as an opportunity to create a new goal: launching a tax planning and tax strategy business for entrepreneurs.

A "wrong" goal is better than no goal because it gives you a direction to move toward. Usually, it's easier to discover that a goal is "wrong" and figure out what your next goal should be when you're in motion, working toward something, not sitting at home worried you'll make a wrong move.

One great way to figure out what you want is to acknowledge what you don't want. I've learned over time that eliminating things I am not interested in doing or having makes some space to discover what does interest me.

3) **I assessed my real priorities.**

You can tell a lot about someone's priorities by looking at their calendar and their bank account. The way I was spending my time and money were not in alignment with what I was actually trying to achieve.

When I assessed how I was spending my time, I found I was more focused on looking busy than on productive work that would help me accomplish my goals.

Every month or so, I'll do a "calendar audit," going over the last 30 days in my calendar to see how I actually spent my time. Each time I do it, I realize how much stuff I was doing that wasn't actually moving the needle toward any of my goals. Then, I can adjust my course so I can make progress. Another happy hour networking event wasn't actually growing my business. It was always the same crowd every night. I could attend half of the events and have the same quantity and quality of connections.

For example, you may notice that you sit with your email inbox open all day and respond to emails seconds after they come in. You look busy and productive, but you're unable to deeply focus on anything else because you always have one eye on the email inbox.

Once, when I did my calendar audit, I realized I was being over-coached. I was spending so much time traveling to various programs and seminars. I was learning great stuff, but I wasn't giving myself a chance to implement it. I needed to reorient how I spent my time so I could actually use the information I learned to move me closer to my goals. After a few months away from coaching and masterminds, the time I spent focused on implementation skyrocketed our business.

4) **I became aware of what I wanted (not what other people wanted for me).**

In the past, I would let my goals and decisions be informed by what I thought other people wanted my life to look like. Now, I know how to tell the difference between what I really want and what I think I "should" want. I realized that my life doesn't have to look like other people's—I have to live my life the way I want to live it.

Have you ever noticed that every town has that one lawyer who always wears a bow tie? For a while, I thought that had to be me. But then I realized that it really wasn't me. Now, I haven't worn a tie (bow or otherwise) for nearly 2 years, and I feel so much more authentic and comfortable.

My parents looked at me sideways when my family started flying first class. That just wasn't something that was done in my family. It was viewed as a waste of money. But after I tried it the first time, and I got to board the plane first, and I actually had leg room, and I had a pretty decent meal while in flight, and my baggage came off of the conveyor first, I realized that there were a lot of benefits to flying that way. It was okay that I was "one of those people."

I live on 16 acres of property and can't see any of my neighbor's houses. Some people come up the driveway and go, "Wow, this must be horrible in the winter" or "Don't your kids want neighbors to play with?" But the people who come up the driveway and say, "Wow, awesome! This is a compound! A fortress!" are the people who truly get me and the people I enjoy spending time with the most. No one will please everyone, but if you live the way you want to live, you'll attract people who appreciate your authenticity. Subdivision life isn't for me, and I'm okay with that (plus, HOA's are horrible).

I used to be so afraid of what people would think of me that I was embarrassed to show signs that I was successful. But as I got older and wiser, I realized that was a stupid way to think. No one is scrutinizing you as much as you think they are. They're too busy worrying about what other people think of them. And if someone is upset that you're successful, what does that say about them?

5) I learned what works for me.

We've all read those productivity articles that outline the "ideal" morning routine for entrepreneurs: wake up at 4am, drink a gallon of water, work out for 2 hours, meditate for an hour, go for a hike, recite your goals 30 times, and then start the day.

There are people who thrive under that structure (who may or may not be total psychopaths). I am not one of those people. And it's bullsh*t to believe there's only one way to achieve success.

I tried so hard to be a member of the "4 am club," but after a while, I had to admit that it wasn't working for me. I prefer to slowly roll out of bed after snoozing six times, take my dog for a walk while I daydream a bit, work out, meditate, drink a smoothie, and start my day at 10am. But at 10:01, I am operating with an enthusiasm unknown to mankind.

We're all wired a little differently, so we have to figure out what works for us. And we can't have any guilt around not fitting into other people's version of what works—that's not productive.

This applies to work styles, too. I discovered I'm great at getting a project started (the first 10%) and at providing leadership in the last 10% of a project. But the part in the middle is not my strong suit. Left to my own devices, without a team, I would probably have 20 unfinished projects that I enthusiastically started and then got bored of. I work best when I have others implement my ideas for me, and then I can show up at the end to ensure it meets my criteria.

I used to feel bad about not working on the middle 80% of projects. But then I realized this wasn't a failure on my part. It was just how I'm wired. Some people are wired to be the ones implementing someone else's vision and would struggle to come up with an idea for a project or provide overarching guidance. They thrive as mercenaries tackling to-do lists and managing projects. (In fact, if you're one of those people, send me your resume. We are *always* hiring). Neither strength is better or more valuable than the other. That's why we need collaboration. We take what I'm best at and what you're best at and put it together so we can accomplish more.

Take time to understand how you operate, and then align everything in your business to that. Become aware of how you work. Maybe you can spend an hour per day on a task. Or maybe you need a full day set aside to tackle that same task. Productivity doesn't look the same for everyone.

I've also learned that I can't work in silence. I focus better in a noisy coffee shop or restaurant. For others, the sound of the air conditioner blowing in a library may be too much of a distraction.

Once you can take these steps, you can really commit to your goals. Will you achieve them? Yes or yes. The choice is yours.

CHAPTER 8

Know Your Numbers

At a certain point in running your business, to get to the next level, you need to know your numbers.

Not having a "number system" is like driving without looking at the dashboard of your car. If you don't check your speed, you'll either take way too long to get somewhere or you'll get a ticket. Plus, your engine may be overheating, or you could be running out of gas.

But it's not realistic to look at all of your numbers all the time. Instead, you'll put systems in place so that when something isn't on track, the red light starts flashing.

You need to carve out time to generate data, process and review it, and create a plan based on it. If you can't find the time yourself, you can assemble a team that can assist you with it. However, as the owner of the business, you can never abdicate this responsibility. It is your responsibility to know these numbers so that you can hold people accountable.

On average, there are about twenty working days in a month. Based on that knowledge, I created a "time budget" for the business. For every category of the business—marketing, management, finances, training, traveling, etc.—how many of those 20 days do I need to spend in each of those categories for the business to grow?

Somewhere in the time budget, I factor in time to track numbers. I've found that as the business has grown, I need to spend more and more time looking at the numbers, and, as a consequence, less and less time doing a job in the business.

Leading vs. Lagging Numbers

It's important to understand the difference between leading indicators and trailing indicators. I can tell now, based on the number of leads we have, how many clients we expect to convert and how much revenue we'll have sixty days from now. For me, "number of leads today" is a *leading indicator* of revenue in 60 days. If I waited to just track revenue, by the time I saw we were falling behind, the dumpster fire would be burning too hot to be extinguished.

Rather than waiting until sixty days from now and saying we don't have enough revenue, I can get ahead of any potential revenue dips by looking at our daily lead flow, and if things dip for more than a few days, I can correct it now, to avoid an impact on revenue. That's how to effectively use leading indicators. But if you only look at the trailing indicator, revenue, after the fact, you miss the opportunity to course correct. Think about what the leading indicators are in your business.

If I'm trying to lose weight, it would be more effective to track the leading indicators of daily calorie intake and minutes exercised than the trailing indicator of pounds I weigh. If I notice that one day I overeat, I can make sure not to repeat that pattern other days and might add an extra workout to stay on track.

The fewer numbers you track as the owner, the better. In a perfect world, I would boil it down to one number that I could check each day to see if the business was headed in the right direction—in my case, that would probably be leads generated. The rest of the team would have access to the data and information in the rest of the business. Fortunately, as your business grows and your team grows, you will have more people for tracking all of that new data that you need.

I ran into another business owner at the gym, and we got to talking about health and fitness. He told me, "As long as I can fit into size 32 pants, I know I'm doing fine." That's his one number. He doesn't have to track macros or count calories to know he's on track with his health goals. If the pants are getting tight, change something. If he can still fit into the size 32s, he can go ahead and have dessert. That is brilliant in its simplicity.

Additionally, if you can designate one number for each employee that provides a simple, at-a-glance indication that they're on the right track, it will be easy to monitor how the business is doing. Our receptionist needs to make sure that 100% of our phone calls get answered. Our sales team needs to make sure they hit our target conversion rate. Our marketing team needs to generate a certain number of leads. They know whether they are successful or not.

If you tried to track 30 numbers a day and manage the business based on that, it would be too complicated, and your team would be confused. The fewer numbers, the better.

You need to know which numbers are important. This is different for every business.

There are now certain numbers in this business that I look at every single day via an email: cash in the bank, number of leads we brought in, and revenue from the day prior.

There are other numbers that I look at weekly: A/R, conversions on leads into clients, billable hours by our staff, and productive hours by our staff. Each department has a weekly scorecard that tracks relevant numbers. There are numbers I look at quarterly, such as the full profit and loss statement and balance sheet, and budget variance.

When we first launched our scorecard, we wanted to track about 20 numbers on a weekly basis as a management team. This was, frankly, too many. We now track 14 numbers on a weekly basis, and of those, only about 10 were on the original list. We learned what really mattered over time. It's important to start tracking rather than waiting to find the perfect numbers to track. If we never started tracking anything, we'd still be driving a car with no gauges. Plus, as the business grows and evolves, the importance of certain numbers, and the frequency with which we check them will change.

If you'd like to see how we structure our scorecard, you can get a template here: https://iamadamwilliams.com/scorecard

Good is Good Enough

If you wait for perfectly accurate data, you're never going to get it, and for most purposes, "close enough" is good enough. For the purposes of decision making, I don't need to know that we spent $1,261.75 on software last month. I just have to know that it was about $1,200 so I can decide if that's how much I want to spend next month. Pursuing the most perfect, accurate number will only slow me down from making decisions.

Trends are more important than absolutes. If you buy an inaccurate scale, you'll still be able to tell whether you're gaining or losing weight based on if the number is going up or down. Of course, there are some numbers where you need to know absolutes (it's probably important to know the minimum cash you need to have in the bank to not panic, and you should get things right on your tax returns, or the financial statements you send to your bank or investors). Even those nerdy accountants have something called a "materiality threshold." If a number is small enough, it's okay if it's inaccurate. But in general, you just need to know if you're trending upward or downward. Our team has struggled with counting "qualified leads" because there's always some dispute about what's "qualified." Once we decided on a consistent definition, the tracking became easier.

And the numbers you track may change over time—keep trying until you get it right. We used to track traffic to our website, but we realized it's a useless metric for us. We'd be better off tracking the leads we generate from the website. If a million people clicked on our website, but none of them signed up for a consultation, it doesn't do us any good, so we needed to focus on tracking those who actually scheduled a consultation. But if you sell ads on your site, traffic may be one of your most important metrics. What's important is different in every business.

The numbers you need to check frequently may change as circumstances change. If our revenue is down, we may need to track the hours our attorneys are working to hold everyone accountable. But if everything is going smoothly, we may not need to track that number for a few months. In a growing business, the amount of working capital (i.e., money in your operating account) increases. If you are growing rapidly, the needs grow rapidly. We use a 16-week cash flow projection so that we can manage revenue and expenses for the next 4 months. We adjust this weekly.

Soon, you'll reach a point where you'll know your numbers so well that you can predict your revenue for the year. Imagine how much easier it is to make decisions when you're able to consistently and reliably predict your numbers. Being able to predict the future gives you peace of mind that you likely never had before.

CHAPTER 9

The Necessity of Hiring Experts

For a long time, I was resistant to the idea of hiring experts. I thought I could figure everything out myself. I'd inherited my dad's mindset of, "I'm intelligent and hardworking…I can do anything I want to do, and usually better than others."

But just because you can do something doesn't mean you have to. Why would I waste a week learning a new skill when I could easily hire someone with a decade of experience in that skill? Well, sometimes there's a good reason. Sometimes I really want to learn a new skill, or sometimes I really enjoy what would be considered a low-value activity (like mowing my lawn). But if I'm doing it for some other reason, I'm probably doing it for the wrong reason.

When I was young, my dad bought a used phone system for his business. Phone systems only have four wires that go into the plugs, and they're four different colors. If you can figure out what each wire does, you can wire your own phone system. I called a phone installer and said, "Can you tell me what the four colors mean? We can figure it out from there." "You can figure it out from there?" the guy said. "No, we're not telling you that." A few calls later, I found a company that was willing to tell us. I wrote down the information, and a few weeks later, my dad had installed his phone system at his store. It worked…most of the time.

Years later, when I moved into my own law office, I got a quote for $1,300 to install Internet cables. "I can do that myself," I thought. So rather than spending time getting clients and growing the firm, I was in the basement, banging my head on pipes, trying to install an internet cable so I could save $1,300.

Five years later, after countless frustrating experiences with the Internet access in the office, I finally caved in and hired a professional to fix what I had done wrong. I never had an Internet issue after that. All it took was that one call to a professional. But because I was too stubborn to hire a professional from the beginning, I endured years of moving my desk closer to the router for Zoom calls so my Internet wouldn't cut out. If I'd spent the money upfront to have it done right by a professional, I could have saved myself that frustration and used the time I wasted installing the internet to grow the firm.

Experts know how to get something done right and get it done quickly. But when you're not the expert, it's unlikely you'll be able to hit both of those marks. You might get it done quickly, but you'll make a mistake that leads to problems in the future. Or you might get it done right, but it takes 10 times longer than an expert would because you have to learn how to do it. When you hire an expert, you can get a task done right and done quickly.

In the early days of starting a business, it can be scary to invest in experts. At the time I installed the Internet, I was terrified of letting go of $1,300 because I thought money was scarce. But over the years, I've learned that business owners can't afford not to hire experts. Time that you spend trying to do something yourself to save money is valuable time wasted that you could use to make a profit and push the business forward. And when the business grows to a certain level, you need to be able to accomplish tasks correctly and quickly. If you don't have experts on your team, you won't be able to keep up. You'll hit a ceiling and never break through.

Hiring experts isn't just limited to hiring outside vendors. Imagine assembling a team of employees who are better at their jobs than you are. It can be done. And rather than facing immense inertia any time you want to get a project started, you have a team pushing you to be better.

When we started our grilled cheese food truck, we hired a professional chef to help us develop the menu. At first, I thought, "Isn't it just two slices of bread and some cheese? How hard can it be? Can't we just do it ourselves?" But I didn't know what I didn't know. It turned out that this chef was experienced in understanding food costs and creating a menu that was both appealing to customers and cost efficient for the business. One of his simple, yet genius, ideas was a grilled cheese sandwich with pickle slaw. It was inexpensive to produce, a hit with customers, delicious... and I would have never thought of it myself. He connected us with suppliers and showed us how to prep the food in a more efficient way. If my team and I had tried to buy different types of bread and cheese and craft the menu ourselves, we would have missed out on a universe of opportunities that we couldn't see because we weren't experts, and we would have been less profitable.

The first time I hired a coaching company to work with our firm, I maxed out my credit card to attend their discovery session and signed a $3,000 a month contract for 18 months. At the time, that was a lot of money to me, so it was a huge investment. It was probably 10% of our monthly revenue. But I knew I just had to make the first month or two work and then the investment would pay off. I was right… Thanks to the coaching service, our business grew much faster than it would have if I tried to go it alone, and I was quickly able to afford the monthly fees. Rather than figuring out everything on my own, they taught me how to work better, and make my business more profitable.

In college, the owner of the painting company I worked for said, "Tiger Woods is the best golfer in the world, but he still hires a golf coach." This quote didn't fully resonate with me until years later, when I was running my own business. I realized he was right. Hiring a coach or an expert doesn't necessarily mean that you lack skill or need help. But we all could use an outside eye to provide guidance and input.

Plus, growth isn't linear. Rather, it usually comes in quantum leaps. You break through to a new level after it feels like you've been stuck for a while. If you work with someone who has been there before, you'll find the instant transformation can be a lot less disruptive.

And sometimes, there's value in someone telling you, "You're on the right track. You've got this." There's a lot of uncertainty when you're running a business, and it can be lonely at the top. It can be encouraging to have a coach to bounce ideas off of and reaffirm your confidence in the steps you're taking.

After realizing the power of investing in experts, I learned to stop sweating the small numbers. I needed to worry about $1,000 an hour decisions, not $1,000 a month decisions. If I wanted to be the owner of a million-dollar business, I needed to let go of my instinct to pinch pennies and realize that small investments are worth it in the long term. Was that easy? Absolutely not. Was it worth it? Absolutely yes.

My frugality was another mindset I inherited from my parents. If we're going out to dinner, my dad will order the fish tacos because it's cheaper than the fish filet. But over the years I've realized that if you want the fish filet, you should go ahead and order the fish filet. We're talking about a difference of a few dollars… Get what you want, and don't sweat the small numbers. It will clear up space in your brain for bigger stuff.

When I was in high school, a car dealership next door to my parents' store went through a remodeling. My dad bought their old sign and it was full of 60-watt light bulbs. Thousands of them. He had it installed on top of his business and programmed it to run different marketing messages. But he went out and bought hundreds and hundreds of 25-watt light bulbs in order to save on the electric bill. He bought cases of these things. So we swapped out the old 60-watt bulbs that still worked, and replaced them with 25's. At the end of the project, we still had a ton of bulbs left over - I think someone miscounted. For years, I never needed to buy a light bulb for my house. In fact, while the rest of the world was moving on to compact fluorescent bulbs, and even LED bulbs, I was still changing the bulbs in my house to the old 60-watters and leftover 25-watters that he bought probably 10 years prior. I'm not sure how much money he saved on that deal. But I knew it took a lot of time and effort to manage that project, and the bulbs took up space at my house, my parents' house, and the business for years. What if he had dedicated that time to constructing a better marketing message for the sign?

I've taken the phrase "it's a lot of money" out of my vocabulary. It's a lot of money…relative to what? If it makes the difference between having what you want and being miserable, is it really a lot of money? It doesn't matter if it's a $30 fish filet or a $25,000 coaching program. If it gets you what you want, it's money well spent. The $1 million yacht sitting in the marina? That's not a lot of money compared to the $50 million yacht in the next slip over. Something is only a lot of money if you compare it to something that costs a lot less. And usually, we are not comparing apples-to-apples.

If you open Zillow and filter by price, it moves in $10,000 increments. $150,000, $160,000, $170,000… But when you hit $1 million, it starts to move in $100,000 increments. $1 million, $1.1 million, $1.2 million… The people who live in $100,000 houses are worried about that incremental $10,000, but the people who live in million-dollar houses are thinking about the incremental $100,000. There's a cause and effect relationship here that most people get backwards. They can afford the million-dollar plus house because they don't worry about small numbers. They're rich because of their perspective and relationship to money and value. Focusing on small numbers will keep you broke.

If you want to be a seven or eight-figure business owner, you have to expand the size of the numbers you're focused on. Don't worry about the small stuff, worry about the big stuff.

It's ironic that it took me so long to accept the idea of hiring experts because I knew the value that my legal expertise provided to others.

I view business partnerships as a marriage. But marriages have a 50% divorce rate, while businesses have an 80% failure rate. We have clients who come to us to establish protections upfront in case the business fails, and we do this by drafting and negotiating partnership agreements or buy-sell agreements. If the business does fail, they're much better off financially and personally because they consulted a legal expert to help them prepare. Some business owners might shy away from this expense, but it will cost them more in the long term if they don't have legal protections and have a conflict with their business partner. And given the odds, this is going to happen 80% of the time.

A lot of clients come to us freaking out because they're getting sued. This is likely the client's first time dealing with a lawsuit, but we're a team of legal experts who has seen hundreds of these cases before. We know ways to quickly resolve, or successfully defend, a lawsuit, and we can use our legal knowledge to find solutions that ease the client's fear and uncertainty.

When you're in a stressful situation such as a "business divorce" or a lawsuit, you sleep better at night knowing an expert will handle it for you. It brings clarity when you have someone with knowledge and experience walking you through a process and filling in the gaps of what you don't know.

And it works the same with the routine operations of the business. It's much less stressful on a day-to-day basis when you know you have a team of experts handling tasks for you.

For a while, I tried to run my own Internet marketing campaigns. We spent a lot of money and got mixed results. Finally, I decided to take the plunge and hire an expert. He creates well-tailored marketing campaigns for us and adjusts them constantly because he knows what the results should look like. I don't have to spend time thinking about Internet marketing other than looking at the reports he brings me, and the marketing pays for itself because it attracts clients.

It's not just a matter of throwing money at a problem. You need to be intentional about the experts you hire. Vet them, get referrals from trusted colleagues, find testimonials, and set clear expectations for your relationship with the expert. But when you find the right expert and learn to collaborate with them to accomplish your goals, it's incredible how much your business can grow.

Hiring an attorney, a good CPA, or a coach, allows you to focus on your business. You didn't start your business so you could figure out how to fill out crappy legal forms you download from the internet (and most of them are really crappy). You started your business to make money, have freedom, and have an impact. Hire an expert so you can get back to focusing on those priorities.

Life is too short to make all of the mistakes on your own. Our businesses benefit from working with business owners who have made a lot of mistakes, and we use that experience to benefit our other clients.

CHAPTER 10

Balance is Bullsh*t

There is a lot of talk, especially in the accounting and legal professions, about work-life balance.

After law school, when I started my career in the tax group at a Big 4 Public Accounting firm, there were articles and trainings about it. It seems like a great idea on its face. Who wouldn't want the scales to be leveled between what's going on in the workplace and what's going on in your personal life?

Here's the problem. It's a complete fantasy. When you achieve work-life balance, *please* fly in on your unicorn and pick me up for dinner with Santa Claus.

It's totally unattainable.

You'll be forever striving for it, without ever achieving it. I found that the most success and happiness in my life comes from intentional imbalance. Here's what I mean by that. There are periods of time when you're not going to see me lift a finger in my business. The obligations and stress are handled by someone else on the team, while I focus on being 100% present with my family or even just by myself. But then when I get back into the office, I'm ready to rock and roll.

On the other hand, if I'm launching an exciting new marketing campaign, or acquiring another business, or we're in the grind of solving difficult challenges in my business, I'm neither surprised nor disappointed when I'm putting in 12 or 14 hour days.

If it were possible to run a business while putting in consistent, predictable hours every single week, it would be a pretty short discussion about work-life balance, because we would just go and do that.

As I write this book, I'm also studying to get my private pilot's license. I want to have the ability to open up my world and travel for business and for pleasure with my family, with a lot more flexibility around scheduling, without the nightmares of crotch-patting airport security and the challenges of having only one direct flight destination out of Erie, Pennsylvania.

I flew to Traverse City, Michigan with my instructor in a tiny old airplane to review the first draft of this book. While we can set the course and the autopilot for our destination, there are lots of things that come up along the way, like weather, wind, or other traffic. There are times during the flight where we can sit back, relax, and enjoy the view, and other times where both my instructor and I have our hands on the controls, our feet on the rudders, and a keen eye out the window making sure no ice is accumulating on the wings.

If life is anything, it's unpredictable, and because of this, you need to be prepared to adjust course, speed, heading, or even altitude as necessary. Heck, there are times you need to make an emergency landing.

As much as I begrudge the hustle and grind culture, I begrudge it because they view hustling and grinding as an end to themselves. Rather, I believe you should hustle and grind if you're working towards something with a definitive finish line. Work for the sake of work is the definition of mindless suffering. Work for the sake of achieving a result is what will bring you true success and freedom.

It's important to be intentional about this. My family understands when I've got to put in the extra time at the office, and the team understands when I'm spending time with my family. Fortunately, both of those parties understand when I need to spend eight or 10 hours a week learning how to fly an airplane. There is no balance there. I think a better word might be living by design. Set your goals and be intentional, work towards them, and enjoy the fruits of your labor.

If the scales are out of balance for too long, I know that I'm heading towards burnout or boredom. It's important to step back every once in a while, get the lay of the land, and decide where I'm heading next. Don't worry, I still haven't beaten this plane analogy to death.

Pilots also remain in constant communication with air traffic control. These outside advisors can let you know what the weather looks like, where it's safe to fly, whether another plane is heading directly on your course, or if a massive jet is going to create some unpleasant turbulence for you.

Even the best pilots in the world have ATC sitting outside the plane in a tower helping them determine where to go. My best experiences with air traffic control are when I can work with them to get to my destination. This is like hiring a coach for your business or any type of advisor—someone outside the cockpit with experience and expertise to help you on a safe and enjoyable journey.

Don't feel guilty when you need to work extra hard or put in extra hours. You still need to be willing to do that. However, there's a difference between working hard all the time and working hard to accomplish a specific goal or outcome. It's okay to have that imbalance for a period of time if you are intentional about it.

When the pandemic hit, Jackie and I hired a nanny for the first time. My son was doing virtual school, and my daughter wasn't yet in preschool. We needed to make sure we had the help we needed so that we could keep the business afloat and show up as the best versions of ourselves for our kids. It can be a real emotional challenge to have someone else watching your kids while you're working from home. You start to question your priorities.

But we laid a foundation during those first few months of the pandemic that supported a business that allowed us to put our kids into the best private school in town, move our family into our dream house with a pool, and take some of the most excellent vacations. If we didn't focus on the business so much back then, we wouldn't be where we are today.

But we had to be mindful about allowing the pendulum to swing back in the other direction. In July 2020, we also bought our first RV. We were able to take memorable trips with our kids and spend real quality time with them. I spent a few weeks working until 2am so that I could spend nights in an RV playing Monopoly with my kids until 2am. I wouldn't trade that for anything.

Free yourself from the belief that you have to achieve balance. Rather, make sure there is a flow or harmony with your work and life.

CHAPTER 11

Entrepreneurial Kids - The Next Generation

Entrepreneurs tend to have entrepreneurial kids. There are exceptions, but in general, if you're an entrepreneur, it's likely your parents were entrepreneurs. And whether your child ends up starting a business or not, you will find that you've passed on entrepreneurial skills that they'll take into the workplace.

Like most parents, I hope my kids do better than I do. I want to intentionally pass on the entrepreneurial skills I had to learn the "hard way" so they can be more successful than I am.

I had an advantage because I had successful entrepreneurial parents. Yeah, it didn't hurt to have a decent family income. But more importantly, I learned lessons and skills that give me the upper hand as an adult. Now, I'm giving my kids an extra leg up, because they've got at least two generations of entrepreneurs who came before them.

I want to teach my kids the value of knowing what you want, being comfortable with what you want, and being willing to say what you want out loud. I didn't learn until later in life that it's okay to want things for your reasons, as long as you have reasons. When you understand this, you have so much freedom and confidence. You become less susceptible to peer pressure and worrying about what other people think.

I also want to instill in them the value of self compassion—forgiving yourself for your mistakes and shortcomings. It's okay to say, "I did the best I could. I could have probably done better. But I'm not going to waste time beating myself up because I could have done better. On to the next one."

There are three "parent behaviors" that I'm trying to remove from my life:

1) Dictating

> How many times have you heard some version of this exchange between a parent and child:
> "Go clean your room."
> "Why?"
> "Because I said so."

Dictating takes away a kid's freedom to think critically. What if you gave them a better answer than "I told you to"? Instead, you could say, "Could you please clean your room? We have guests coming over, and you'll probably want room to play, and you'll want to know where your toys are." This explanation teaches the kid something about life and helps them develop critical thinking skills. They understand the reasoning behind doing what you told them to do. By dictating, you take away their ability to think critically.

2) Bribing

When you bribe a kid, you're offering them things that they don't necessarily want. It's just what you think they want.

You're taking away their ability to decide what they want for themselves. I could bribe my daughter to put laundry away by saying, "I'll give you $20." But it gives her much more freedom if I say, "I want you to put away the laundry. What would you like in exchange for that?" She gets to consider what she really wants rather than just accepting my version of what I think she wants. At this point, she'd probably say she wants a new toy—she loves unboxing a new toy and playing with it for ten minutes just for the joy of discovery. Or maybe she just wants to spend time with me watching a movie or playing a game. If you don't let your kids build the muscle of deciding what they want, they'll grow into adults who find it hard to determine what they want and are too easily swayed by what other people want from them.

3) **Overcompensating**

Overcompensating looks like, "Take out the trash and I'll give you $50" or "You got straight A's this quarter? Let's go to Disneyland!" Some parents totally destroy their kid's perception of the value of things. They become spoiled and expect rewards to come too easily. The first millennial I hired asked for a raise within 30 days of working for me. I told him, "You've done nothing yet, we're still training you." But he had parents who overcompensated, so he thought he was entitled to a reward before he'd earned it. He had little patience, and he lacked a real understanding of getting paid for the value he provided.

When a kid turns into an entitled adult, it's usually the parent's fault for creating an environment where the kid was given an outsized reward they didn't deserve. These kids become impatient when they enter the real world and discover that rewards only come from results.

More parents need to embrace the idea of seeing their kids achieve their own definition of success. I see so many parents impose their own definitions of success on their kids. We've all seen that one dad at the Little League game who loses his mind when his kid strikes out because he wants his kid to be perfect to make up for his own insecurities. Or we all know people who chose career paths purely to please their parents. But parenting is about giving your kids the foundation to achieve their own versions of success. It may not look like yours, and that's okay.

When I was younger, I had an idea of success that meant a nice house, a flashy car, and a lot of money in the bank. It was about proving to other people that you'd achieved success. Now, I've developed my own definition of success that's about having time freedom from the business and having a positive impact on other entrepreneurs. It turns out that financial success is a byproduct of that, but it's not the end goal. I was raised to think that hard work was the highest form of achievement. Now, I realize that building a business that allows me to take time off is what I really desired as success.

Money is an easy way to measure success because it's a number, but it wasn't until I got older that I realized there are other ways to measure success.

I hope that my kids create their own definitions of success and are able to achieve it. I also hope they're willing to allow that definition to evolve over time. Success for me at age 40 looks different than it did at age 30. There are things I wanted then that I don't want now, and that's okay. Although, there's still that 19-year-old version of me that shops for private islands on the Internet.

Kids learn from what you do much more than from what you say. If your kids see you live as an entrepreneur according to your values and achieve your own version of success, it'll make an impact on them.

You've gotten this far. Congratulations. It's time for your journey to continue.

I expect some lawyer to read this and send me a nasty email because I promised to teach "everything" your kids wish you knew about running a business so that you can have a better life for them. But if you read this far, it's because you got value out of this book. You understood the lessons, and you are ready to start testing them in your life and business. If you are ready to supercharge that transformation, my team and I are ready to help.

ABOUT THE AUTHOR

Every book on entrepreneurship tells you to hire a good accountant and a good lawyer. Attorney Adam Williams started his law practice to be that lawyer for entrepreneurs. Building off of that success, with a firm of over 20 people, Adam has helped launch other startups with both a local and national impact.

It only took 12 years for Adam to become an overnight success. He now spends his time managing the law firm, aggressively pursuing more growth through creative marketing and business acquisitions, and avoiding the eye rolls in the office as he cracks more dad jokes.

After growing his law firm to multiple seven figures, Adam began speaking more frequently, coaching other entrepreneurs, and scaling other businesses.

Adam provides countless valuable resources to entrepreneurs at his website www.IAdamAdamWilliams.com.

Made in the USA
Monee, IL
18 June 2024

572bb6b3-fe68-40f7-aa1c-55edf63ca094R01